after the oracle

AFTER THE ORACLE,

or: How the Golden State Warriors'
Four Core Values Can Change Your Life
Like They Changed Mine

Shane Anderson

DEEP VELLUM PUBLISHING
DALLAS, TEXAS

Deep Vellum Publishing
3000 Commerce St., Dallas, Texas 75226
deepvellum.org · @deepvellum

Deep Vellum is a 501c3 nonprofit literary arts organization
founded in 2013 with the mission to bring
the world into conversation through literature.

ISBNs: 978-1-64605-146-5 (paperback) | 978-1-64605-147-2 (ebook)

LIBRARY OF CONGRESS CATALOGING-IN-PUBLICATION DATA:
Names: Anderson, Shane, author.
Title: After the oracle; or, How the Golden State Warriors' four core
values can change your life like they changed mine / Shane Anderson.
Other titles: After the oracle
Description: Dallas, Texas : Deep Vellum Publishing, 2021.
Identifiers: LCCN 2021019907 (print) | LCCN 2021019908 (ebook) | ISBN
9781646051465 (hardback) | ISBN 9781646051472 (ebook)
Subjects: LCSH: Self-actualization (Psychology) | Joy. | Mindfulness
(Psychology) | Compassion. | Competition. | Coaching (Athletics)
Classification: LCC BF637.S4 A6114 2021 (print) | LCC BF637.S4 (ebook) |
DDC 158.1--dc23
LC record available at https://lccn.loc.gov/2021019907
LC ebook record available at https://lccn.loc.gov/2021019908

Cover Design by Vytautas Volbekas
Interior Layout and Typesetting by KGT

PRINTED IN THE UNITED STATES OF AMERICA

For Melanie—and for Kian,
who came after

One does not need to imagine that lemon; one needs to discover it.
—Jack Spicer, poet

You can speak about spirit, or you can live it.
—Jürgen Klopp, coach

CONTENTS

Beginning, Again

That's it, I thought. *We've lost*. I pushed my office chair away from my desk in frustration. Then rolled backwards with my hands on top of my head and groaned. My chair hit my bed and I spun around to look at the alarm clock on the dilapidated Art Deco nightstand I had found on the street last week. *Scheiße*, I said. It was almost 6:00 AM here in Berlin. Way past an even indecent hour to go to bed but also too early to fall asleep; I had to see whether my favorite basketball team, the Golden State Warriors, were really going to lose this final game of the 2009–10 regular season.

Our odds looked awful even though we were technically winning, 108–104. The Warriors' Devean George had just fouled out with 4:47 left in the final quarter and there were no healthy players on the bench to replace him. I didn't know what would happen but guessed we would be forced to forfeit. I cursed under my breath, this time in English, and a smirk emerged on my lips. *It figures*. We always lost. It was our destiny. With but a few notable exceptions, the Warriors had been an awful team since long before I devoted myself to them in elementary school in the late 1980s. And this year hadn't been any different. We had already lost 56 of the 81 games we had played, often very badly. Tonight's inevitable loss really stung, though. We had actually had a chance against the Portland Trail Blazers, a team headed to the play-offs—unlike us, who were headed to the NBA draft lottery like all the other bottom feeders.

I pinched the bridge of my nose and adjusted my glasses. *Come on,* I thought, *who knows?* Still seated and crab walking back to the computer screen, I listened to the Warriors' broadcasters detail some NBA legalese that would allow George to stay in the game. The camera cut to Don Nelson, the Warriors' head coach, who was arguing with the referees, pleading for the game to continue. I watched him raise his eyebrows and shake his head then looked out the window of my studio apartment. The sky was already bright and blue and the horse chestnut in the courtyard was in bloom. I did a quick mental calculation. If it was 6:00 AM here, it was 9:00 PM in Portland, Oregon, where the game was being played. And if it was April 14, 2010, on the West Coast, then tomorrow here would be the 16th, my birthday, which I dreaded. It would be my second birthday alone and the fifth one in this foreign country I now called home.

I started feeling anxious. Like I needed to smoke. I walked into the kitchenette, opened the window, lit a cigarette. While I watched my breath dissolve over the quiet courtyard, I thought about Portland, the city my sister lived in, and about my sister, whom I hadn't spoken to in years. The last time we connected was when she was living in Alaska, working on a fishing boat. I had heard she was now studying fish management at a community college in Oregon, since when I didn't know. I wondered whether I should check in with her or if she would write for my birthday. I knew she wouldn't. Everyone was still mad at me for what had happened. And I didn't want to have anything to do with any of them, either. Not after everything that had happened before. I inhaled some more smoke, then exhaled and turned my thoughts to what just happened on the court.

The Warriors had started the game with only six players healthy enough to play: the five starters (Stephen Curry, Monta Ellis, Chris Hunter, Anthony Tolliver, and Reggie Williams) and George, who would only come off the bench in case of emergency. Unfortunately, the Warriors had to cash out that insurance policy pretty fast. Hunter injured himself in the first quarter, and the rest of the Warriors, now down to the absolute minimum of players, would have to play a perfect game for its remainder. No fouling out, no injuries, no ejections. And they did, coming back from a ten-point deficit and demonstrating heart and grit. But now George had to exit and there was no way we could win with only four players on the court.

I closed the kitchenette window, walked back to my desk, and saw Hunter hobbling to the scorers' table.

What's going on? They're not going to make him play with a bum leg, are they?

They were.

The game started again. And Hunter blocked a shot on the first possession. I started rooting for my team, I could feel the positive effects it was having, the hope that was blossoming. But then the Warriors missed their next shot and Hunter fouled a Blazer on the next defensive possession. An and-1 that was even worse since he also reinjured his leg. He hobbled back off the court and we were back at the beginning.

Now what?

Timeout, Golden State.

I looked out at the blossoms again, at the tree that would produce horse chestnut seeds, poisonous if eaten. I thought about buying curtains, also to sleep better in the daytime. In the background I could hear the Blazers' home crowd turning from impatient to apoplectic. Their boos were becoming architectural in dimension, towering over the Warriors' broadcasters. Worried about waking my neighbors, I muted the feed I was illegally streaming then watched Nelson yell what I guessed were obscenities at the referees in silence. I watched hundreds of fans stand up and threaten him, incensed about this ridiculous ending, which was also frustrating me. I was tired. I opened another browser tab to look for curtains at IKEA, too expensive, then eBay, too ugly. I considered going to bed but grabbed a beer from the half-sized fridge instead. When I came back to my desk and clicked on the game's tab, I saw Ronny Turiaf walking onto the court. I unmuted the computer. The Warriors' broadcasters reminded the viewers that Turiaf was injured but that he had suited up because of some arcane NBA regulation—a team needs at least eight players in uniform to compete—and now would have to play. I thought it was cruel of the referees to not back down from the stringency of the law, but I didn't expect anything less.

The game started again.

Then stopped again.

Turiaf immediately committed an offensive foul and feigned a new injury.

He left the game and the referees made Anthony Morrow check in.

Morrow, the other inactive active Warrior player, performed the same charade.

The game started, then stopped, when Morrow "hurt himself" as Ellis casually fouled a Blazer on the next possession.

What's going on? I thought.

Why are we doing this?

It seemed like some mad-hat endgame strategy where we were willing to give up all of our pieces, but I wasn't sure what it was for.

Now we were down 108–109 with 3:38 left to play and only four Warriors still on the court.

The broadcast cut to a commercial break in this never-ending game.

I took a sip of beer; an SUV advertisement aired in the background. I opened another tab and looked at the league standings on nba.com. I couldn't believe what I was seeing. It would actually be better to lose. A loss tonight would mean falling in the standings and falling in the standings would mean that our record would be worse than the Kings, and that would mean we would be projected to draft DeMarcus Cousins, a center from Kentucky who could provide inside scoring and strength and finesse like we hadn't seen from a center since the 1980s, and that would mean we might actually stop losing all the time, it would mean we would change our destiny. I started praying for the Warriors to lose. *Please, just think about the future.*

The broadcast came back and I clicked on the tab.

George was now walking to the scorers' table, but we would

be assessed a technical foul so that he could re-enter. A small price to pay to be able to finish the game.

We were still down 108–109 with 3:38 left in regulation.

The game started again.

And that's when the magic began.

The Blazers' Patty Mills made the technical free throw, 108-110, then missed his next two shots from the line for the foul Ellis had committed against him ages ago, when Morrow was on the court. George grabbed the rebound from the second miss and passed the ball to Curry. Curry brought the ball up the court and sunk a jumper from the baseline. It was all tied up 110-110 with 3:19 to go. The game started picking up its pace. Blazers forward Nicolas Batum missed a three and Curry rebounded, sticking in his own pull-up three from the wing, 113-110, 2:46 left in regulation. I retracted my hopes of losing and started rooting for my team. The Blazers missed another shot, then Curry hit a guarded step-back jumper from the elbow. It seemed like the Blazers had gone cold during that endless debate over the rulebook. The game went back and forth, points were scored. Then the Blazers fouled Curry, who made two free throws, and then they fouled Anthony Tolliver, who made two more. We were winning. The Blazers missed again and fouled Curry again, and again he made both of his free throws. One more foul and the game was over. Final score: 122-116.

We won.

We should have lost, but we won.

We won!

In what was now the early morning of April 15, 2010, in Berlin, the Warriors' players were celebrating on the court like they had won the championship and I was celebrating in front of my screen. I pumped my fist and loudly yelled *Yes*—then remembered the neighbors. The Warriors had actually won, and Stephen Curry had just performed a miracle, scoring eleven of his now-career-high 42 points in the final minutes.

This kid is incredible, I thought. *We're so lucky to have him.* The rookie Curry practically carried the exhausted team on his inexperienced back, and he seemed to be having a lot of fun doing it. What was more, he made it all seem so effortless.

Which, if I thought about it, was actually depressing.

Like most fans, I identified with my team, and had since before I could think. Raised in South Lake Tahoe, California, I was born into a family that had been Oakland sports fans since the 1960s. Raiders games were church for us in the fall and winter and we always made pilgrimages to watch the A's play baseball in the East Bay's pleasant summer. For two special birthdays in a row, my father even spoiled me by allowing me to ditch school so that we could go see the Warriors during the heyday of RUN TMC, that electrifying team featuring Tim Hardaway, Mitch Richmond, and Chris Mullin. You could say then that I fell into the fold of worshipping the team in Oakland, despite the Sacramento Kings being geographically closer, and I proudly sported my Warriors Starter parka to school on cold winter mornings. But now I realized that I couldn't fully identify with this terrible team and not just because I was even further away, sitting in my apartment on the other side of the world. Unlike the Warriors, I didn't have reserves of strength like the ones they had just demonstrated against the Trail Blazers, and, what was worse, no part of me could muster Curry's pre-pubescent-looking swagger. I could never be as great as Stephen Curry: my life has never felt that effortless. Instead, I was a jobless recent divorcée living in a foreign country, who was tired, anxious, and distant while I failed to recover from a psychotic upbringing and major back surgery. Which is a lot to handle in a single sentence and even more when every day proves to be a struggle that you know you are going to lose, painfully and in humiliation.

So, sitting at my desk in my studio apartment in Berlin's Neukölln district, I stopped making comparisons. I wasn't fortunate enough to be as gifted as Curry and I wasn't willing to put in the work to make something of whatever talents I maybe had hidden. I tried to remind myself that life is not basketball. It's a game where the objective is to score more points than your opponent by putting a ball through a ring. Basketball, I mean. Looking at sports as a metaphor for life's complex relations seemed to be an oversimplification of the clusterfuck called the world and it was therefore unfounded.

It would take almost a decade for me to fully believe I was wrong back then. Until I felt that basketball could provide a worthy frame to put your picture in, and that by doing so you can discover aspects that would have otherwise remained hidden. But I'm getting ahead of myself. And by getting ahead of myself, I am letting you know that we're going to get to a place after 250-some-odd pages in this story—about me and other people and the Golden State Warriors and homelessness and a number of other things—where the game will not feel arbitrary to living and where we will realize that we're all in this together.

This is a sentiment that would have felt totally corny if not a deliberate distortion or injustice to me in 2010. Which brings us back to the beginning.

* * *

At home in the early morning, I segued from the basketball game into what I did every night that turned into day. I went into my studio apartment's kitchenette, diminutive even for its formal designation, and grabbed another beer from the half-sized fridge. I cracked it open with a lighter and put the new bottle cap on the empty bottle. Then I leaned halfway out the kitchenette's window and smoked another cigarette. Afterward, I sat down at the oversized slab of plywood that served as my desk and closed the illegal streaming site's window, a refresh arrow's looping back gesture where the game's action had been. I checked my emails.

Awaiting me was an unread message from my ex-wife's grandfather, who had written from his home in the Black Hills of South Dakota at 11:55 CET. I had emailed him yesterday on the pretense of asking his opinion about the Japanese writer Yasunari Kawabata while casually slipping in a question about "Grace," who was not answering my emails. My ex-wife's grandfather responded with a cursory recollection of what the Japanese author had meant to him when he was stationed in Japan after the War but avoided my question about Grace, who had moved in with her grandparents after our breakup in Berlin almost two years ago.

Sitting now in the morning light, I looked out the lone window in the main room of the studio apartment and saw the horse chestnut blossoms in the courtyard. I followed my fingers to where they always went whenever I thought about Grace: the URL of the Flickr account she administrated during our time together. The internet knew where I wanted to go almost before I did; the address was predicted, then autofilled, and the page was opened. I saw the few pictures of our old apartment in Reuterkiez as well as the beginning of our immoderately documented wedding in 2008. These first few pages weren't why I visited the account, however. For more than a month, I'd been coming here to find the exact moment when I knew we shouldn't get married on the Ides of March, a day historically known for betrayal.

I randomly clicked on page seven at the bottom of the feed. There I discovered a handful of flash photos that Grace had snuck in the Louvre in 2007. An overexposed photo of Rembrandt's painting of a slaughtered ox was followed by a photo of me standing in some nook of the museum, glaring out the window. With my hands on my hips and wearing the grey H&M sweater that had never fit, I was accidentally posing like the unfocused sculpture behind me, tilting its head back, grimacing. Whether the sculpture was in the throes of anguish or ecstasy was difficult to say, but I attributed my expression of discomfort to the normal level of lower back pain I experienced after walking around for a day, ever since I had a major back surgery in 2005. In the next picture, Grace looked happy.

I kept scrolling.

Further down were pictures from the Versailles gardens, close-ups of a Louis XIV-era candelabra, as well as architectural details from the Grande Mosquée de Paris, all from that same April holiday for my birthday. But this page didn't help me find why we shouldn't have gotten married, so I navigated to page 11. We were in Greece. I was standing on top of the Acropolis in August 2006, this time for Grace's birthday. With my arms crossed over my chest, I was totally disgruntled about something.

Then, three photos later, my arms were uncrossed, and the profile of my face was smiling at the Mediterranean. Two photos later, I was kissing Grace's cheek while she took a primitive selfie with her SSLR on a ferry to Crete.

I took another swig of beer in my studio apartment, finished it, grabbed another one from the kitchenette, then went back to my desk. I clicked through page after page, scrolling through all the contradictory displays of emotion. I found a tentative answer to the question "When would have been a good time to stop?" as far back as page 14, a trip to Chamonix with our friends from California. In one of the pictures, time-stamped at 11:42 AM on January 31, 2006, I'm hugging a post that pointed toward Berlin on top of the snow-covered mountain. My eyes were a challenge. I never wanted to go "home."

Just then, the garbage collectors battered the large containers in the courtyard of my apartment building and the clatter echoed up to the German fourth-floor, my window that was tilted open. It disrupted my train of thought and meant that it was much later, or earlier, in Berlin than it should be. I closed the window, the window on my computer's browser as well as the machine. I went to bed.

To avoid thinking about myself, I thought about the Warriors game that just ended. Why couldn't we just lose to the Portland Trail Blazers? There was no shame in tanking. Now our draft pick would fall somewhere in the middle of the lottery and we would lose our chance to draft DeMarcus Cousins. Nelson knew we needed Cousins to replace Biedriņš as our starting center! Biedriņš was always injured and totally useless! But then it seemed like Nelson desperately wanted to win, I guess to cement his record as the winningest coach in NBA history. It was a rather selfish decision. Typical Nelson! Ever since we had experienced the ecstasy of the "We Believe" year in 2007, where we had far excelled expectations with a group of misfits, Nelson had turned into a total curmudgeon and had alienated all of our players. Everyone left! And we ended up with nothing! I hated Nelson! I weirdly started crying. All the selfishness and deceit and loneliness and losing and abandonment and stupidity were getting to me. I tried to pull myself together. Then, I prayed in anger. Please God, let the owner finally sell the Warriors! Or at least fire Nelson! It was time to start over. I paused on this sentence. I stopped crying. Then started even more.

I remember nothing after this.

When I woke up later that day, the sun was streaming through the window, which I tilted open. I walked into the kitchenette and poured a sachet of magnesium powder into a glass of water for my hangover. As I admired the Eurasian jay sitting in the horse chestnut in the early afternoon, I decided to treat myself to an early birthday present. I put on my glasses, gathered my swimming things, and left the house immediately.

In front of my door, I discovered a small pool of blood that was almost finished drying. I locked my door from the top and bottom then knocked on the door of my neighbor across the hall. Kayvan, I yelled in German, we've got junkies again, keep your ears open. He turned down the news that was constantly streaming from his apartment and said, *Mach ich*.

Walking down the stairs, I saw drops of fresh blood for two floors. I was agitated and then distracted from this when I walked into the front building's main entryway. Near the door was a box of things with a sign that read *zu verschenken*. I held up a pair of pants that didn't fit as well as a t-shirt that had blood on it, then walked out the door. I licked my teeth and realized I hadn't brushed them before leaving again. Then I walked past the Turkish bakery, the erotic Thai massage parlor, the internet cafe, the organic store, and toward the bike repairman who was standing in the door to his shop. Beautiful day, I said. He agreed. But why wasn't I out on my old Peugeot? Had it finally crapped out on me? I told him that one of the loose spokes had caused another flat on the back tire, but that it didn't matter. I liked walking. *Is ja jut*, he said in his thick Berliner accent, knowing that I couldn't afford his services.

I walked past the pharmacy on the corner to Hermannstraße then past the cheap German bakery. I smiled at the mothers wearing headscarves who were pushing their children in strollers out of the drugstore. Then I laughed at the photo store's unfortunate new advertisement—"BABY SHOOTING, AB 33€"—and entered the U-Bahn at Boddinstraße.

For the first time in months, I purchased a ticket from the machine. Normally, I rode the nine stations to Rosenthalerplatz on the U8 line illegally, only to stand inside the door of the moving train, scanning the platforms as the train entered the next station, looking for groups of undercover ticket controllers who fanned out to separate doors. But today, I got on with my stamped ticket, calm and not focused on the doors.

I was excited inside the pool's foyer. It was going to be a real treat to swim my 1500-meter routine with light pouring through the glass ceiling above it, and I didn't mind spoiling myself for my birthday by paying for the daytime rate. At the ticket counter, the woman recognized me from when I used to swim in the afternoons as a student, those years where I would leave the Bertolt Brecht archives or the Humboldt Universität library and walk through Mitte to do my doctor's prescribed laps. *One student ticket?* she asked. Actually, I'll have a *Zehner Karte*, I said, testing my luck. Without even asking to see my student ID that hadn't been valid for three years, she printed up the ticket that was good for ten entries at the discounted rate and laminated it. I paid, relishing how much money I would be saving and the fact that I could swim whenever I wanted. I thanked the woman for the early birthday present but used other words.

The day only got better when I entered the pool's locker room, took off my shoes, and found that my favorite locker was still available. Exactly halfway down the center row of lockers on the right-hand side, number 158 was the perfect distance between the showers and entryway. You would never get too cold on your long walk to the end of the lockers when you came out of the showers after swimming, and you would never have to stand in someone's else drippings at the beginning of the lockers when you changed. With a minimal amount of water on the ground, you could walk all the way from the entrance to 158 without getting your socks soggy.

After getting undressed and locking up my belongings, I went into the showers. Without my glasses on, I had to squint to see whether the third shower from the end was free. Number 3, as I liked to call it, had the longest spring of all the showers, which meant the water would keep running for almost longer than you wanted when you pressed the button. Naked and with my goggles wrapped around my wrist, I walked over to Number 3. I did my stretches under the jets and was pleased to discover that I had no shoulder pain to speak of.

Regular discomfort in my shoulder was a small price to pay for the major corrective surgery I had in 2005 for scoliosis. After years of my spine slowly warping into a question mark, the doctors had stretched it out and installed two metal rods along the length of my vertebrae, drilling a handful of two-inch screws into my body. This new "hardware" would serve as permanent scaffolding for my newly fused vertebrae, the thirteen individual bones that were now united, melded into one, even after the hardware no longer served a function. The procedure had been an overwhelming success—I even grew two inches from the procedure and was finally a decent height for a small point guard at 6'2"—and my only prescribed physical therapy was to walk every day and swim three times a week. There was, however, one odd complication. When I woke up in the recovery room, I was very lucid but then slipped back under the narcosis. Having already removed the breathing tube, the nurses were forced to reinsert the plastic into my now swollen throat, scratching my vocal cords. Awake again, without the tube, I noticed my voice was different. It was higher than before—more rattled, unable to hold a note. I had lost the voice that was my own.

The jets of Number 3 finished. I put on my Speedo and walked onto the calm pool deck, whose waters were welcoming the blue sky streaming through the glass roof above. I set down my bag of toiletries in front of the row of heaters at the far end of the pool then licked my goggles. I pulled them over my eyes and inserted my earplugs.

My first 500 meters of freestyle passed without any negative pings from my shoulder and I pounded my way through the five alternating 100s of breaststroke and backstroke. When I finished my final 500 of freestyle, I squinted at the clock and felt like I had made record time, perhaps less than twenty-eight minutes. I draped my towel over my shoulders and removed my earplugs. I felt eyes lasered on the thin incision along the length of my back that turned purple from the cold. From the corner of my eye, I could see a child indecorously pointing at me. I turned around just as his father slapped his hand away.

Walking past them, I heard the father say in German that I probably had an accident. When his son asked why, the father replied people are unlucky sometimes. Frazzled, I stopped in my tracks. I considered turning back. But what could I say to contradict him? It wasn't an accident? It was a condition?

After standing under Number 3 for at least four pushes of the button, I worked up the courage to confront him. How dare he say I was unlucky! He didn't even know me! He had no right to make any claim on my providence! Besides, I thought, I am lucky. I had just saved a ton of money on the *Zehner Karte*! I started cussing under my breath and I thought I would even be ready to push him if he talked back but then his child came around the corner and smiled at me without a tinge of pity.

After leaving the pool as quickly as possible, I walked down Gartenstraße and across Torstraße to the kiosk, the *Späti*. I bought a beer and decided to walk home to blow off some steam even though my hair was still wet and it wasn't very warm. I went down Kleine Hamburgerstraße, turned left before the soccer field, then continued past rows of Soviet-era housing blocks and the squat next to the graveyard on Linienstraße. I walked all the way to Rosa-Luxemburg-Platz, then bought another beer at another *Späti*. Unlucky. I just spent fifteen cents less at this kiosk than the one before it. I walked past the Volksbühne and smoked a cigarette, then turned left on Memhardstraße. After I downed the rest of the beer, I bought another one at the kiosk there, which had a large group of late-middle-aged men with Rewe shopping bags, grumbling on *Bierbänke*. I spent the same amount of money as the last time and felt assured in my convictions that I was definitely not unlucky. Then I continued onto Alexanderplatz, past the Russian punks sitting outside of Galeria Kaufhof, who were petitioning for money for cocaine, LSD, weed, and vodka on four different signs, each with a tattered paper coffee cup behind them. I applauded their honesty and kept walking, past the able-bodied man sitting in a wheelchair who was selling Bratwurst for a Euro from the grill that was attached to the wheelchair. I sneered at him and his misuse of medical equipment then took another swig in front of the grimy, Soviet-era water fountain in the center of the square. I finished my beer and gave it to a bottle collector, an old lady who could make eight cents at the kiosks for each one, then took the photo of a Polish couple, who petitioned me to get the TV tower into the picture as well. After I gave them their camera back, I continued down Alexanderstraße, along the length of the new shopping mall Alexa, and into the wastelands before Jannowitzbrücke.

This space in the middle of the city had been laid barren after a bomb had decimated whatever was here before the Second

World War and I always felt uncomfortable passing this desolate lot. Today I almost ran past it. The space was definitely unlucky. Crossing the bridge over the river Spree, I saw an on-duty police officer stretching his quads in front of the Chinese Embassy as well as people doing Tai Chi on the other side of the bridge, protesting China's humanitarian injustices.

I kept walking, then bought another beer across the street from the dive bar Melancolia I. I hopped on the U8 at Heinrich-Heine-Straße, and rode two stops to Kottbusser Tor, where it was more likely that a team of ticket controllers would enter. Out of the U-Bahn, I passed the crowds of young Turkish men standing around the evening vegetable stand at Kotti and I listened to the vegetable sellers spoken song for discounted groceries. I smoked a cigarette as I walked down Kottbusserstraße, then bought another beer on Kottbusserdamm. I rode the train the two stops from Schönleinstraße to Boddinstraße, pounded the remainder of the beer, and walked into the Vietnamese restaurant Jasmin Bistro. I had probably already spent at least half of my savings from the *Zehner Karte* on beer but I didn't care. The friendly waitress asked me, *Wie immer?* and I nodded my drunken and tired head. Yes, 26a—the tofu in peanut curry sauce, with a large Berliner Kindl. Thank you.

When I woke up, the lights were still on and my beer was mostly full, and it was late morning. Thankfully, I found my glasses lying next to me and not gnarled beneath me like last time. My teeth felt furry after more than a day of not brushing them, so I went into the bathroom. I brushed my teeth under the shower, then sang "Happy Birthday" to myself.

I dried off and opened my email full of expectation, but no one had written to congratulate me on being born into this body. Blame was easy to place on the fact that most of my friends and family were still sleeping on the West Coast of America, but that was a lie. No one wanted to have anything to do with me since I left Grace. No one had written last year except Luciano and Grace, who wrote at almost midnight exactly, Berlin time, although she was already in South Dakota.

With no email from Grace but with Grace unavoidably in my mindspace, I entered the URL for the Flickr account and scrolled down to a picture that caught my eye. Her boss from the language school in Berlin was sitting with her boyfriend at a glass patio table at our wedding reception. Grace and I often went to clubs with them to do ecstasy—in fact, Grace had proposed to me in Berghain while we were peaking—but I didn't want them to be at the wedding, I didn't particularly like them. I then grimaced and remembered a moment that was not documented in our Flickr account. One day when we were already back in California to prepare for the wedding, I discovered that Grace had presented me a truncated version of the guest list. Against my wishes, she had in fact invited her boss as well as my racist uncles, people with whom I didn't want to celebrate. And then she lied to me with a fake list of invitees.

Unlike in the years prior to the discovery of this deception—when we would argue about whether we wanted to live in Berlin or the Bay Area or, God forbid, if we wanted to have children, while we sat in the inexpensive pensions that guidebooks had recommended in Athens and Paris—I did not scream or get angry on this occasion. The voice that was no longer my own went silent. I was resigned to everything. Maybe I mumbled something about the fact that our agreed-upon reasons for getting married had been bureaucratic and fiscal and that the dimensions of the wedding were becoming more like the real thing, and maybe she insisted that if we were going to throw a party we might as well throw a good one, but I couldn't remember. There are so many gaps to live with.

I couldn't breathe. I walked away from my desk, smoked a cigarette, then went back and opened a new browser window. My fingers hovered above the search bar then I entered the Flickr URL again, even though it was open in another tab. I saw myself smiling in a picture and knew I was faking it. I remembered how desperately I had tried to work myself into my role of the groom-to-be, convincing my brain I was doing the right thing. The dominating, despotic fear of not being the person I thought everyone wanted me to be had stopped me from hearing any of my friends' cryptic suggestions that I didn't have to do anything, that I could just stop before I did any more damage. Getting a small whiff of this, I would chalk up my fear to cold feet, something countless other happy couples had gone through. When the day arrived, I would be ready. I just needed the stage in order to play my role more convincingly.

In the weeks before the wedding, I had an occasional flash of prescience, of knowing that something terrible was coming and that I didn't identify with my chosen character. I mostly existed in a prolonged dawn of almost and was too afraid to not fulfill my duty. I was also afraid of hurting Grace and too blind to realize that by staying together only out of a sense of duty to the person who had taken care of me after my surgery, I was only making matters worse for her and for me and for any sense of justice or decency I had, if any.

Four days before the wedding, my body started rebelling against the cruelty of my reason. I broke out in hives and the doctor said it was either syphilis or psychosomatic. The test results were definitive. It wasn't syphilis.

My body was telling me to stop with its own language.

I didn't listen, choosing to repeat a mantra of "I can't go on. I will go on." I couldn't disappoint my parents, who were happy for me for the first time in forever, or any of the people who had flown in from all over the world, whether I wanted them to or not. I was desperately scared. Of doing the wrong thing, of losing everything. But I was also full of rage—blind and blinding and wanting to blind. I tried to keep that inside me and often failed.

I refreshed my email, praying for a little warmth from someone.

My inbox was empty.

I felt like I was being strangled.

It was suddenly there.

The hard plastic corset I had worn around my core after the surgery.

The one that protected my oversensitive nerve endings, organs, and hardware from any of the world's potential thumps.

Thick and obtrusive, this shell had kept me from getting that deep, intoxicating hit of oxygen when you summon up the courage to speak the words that make your lips quiver, the words you suppress because it is easier or more convenient or kinder or maybe not even true, just a fleeting moment of anger or fear.

These are the words that destroy you if they go unspoken. They are the words that become silent spells, where you hex yourself and the magic begins to do what it does, eating your intestines, clogging your lungs, and turning your hair grey from the anxiety of no longer being able to say the words you contain, the words that contain you.

I don't love you.

And probably never did.

I was back in the present.

Living in Berlin without direction.

The shell was swallowing me.

Out of defiance, I wrote:

"I've always had this feeling that life has somehow dragged me by the ear and that all of the things that I've wanted to do were somehow disallowed, that it would only mean more pain and strife if I did what I really wanted. I then had this dual attitude of resigning myself to this fact by just letting things happen and being resentful to the person or thing that always seemed to make everything else impossible. I guess what it boils down to was that I thought I was all very self-aware and honest with my emotions but in reality I was very unclear. I treated you poorly . . . I'm sorry."

Then saved this unsent message in my drafts folder and answered Grace's grandfather instead. I thanked him for his friendship. And meant it. But also knew I would never write him again.

* * *

These three days were a cardboard cutout for the three years to come. They had all the right features but lacked the depth of repeated misery and I am unable to do justice to this misery, as I remember less than I've forgotten—some days were just numb. Willingly passed over then, unwillingly now. I resigned myself to loneliness and estrangement even as I tried to fight it off with beer and basketball and cigarettes and the conversations I had three afternoons a week at St. George's Bookshop, where I started working part-time in September 2010. All of these filled a hole, but the hole was more like a slot for a coin in a ticket machine that kept spitting the coins back out.

But then—I'm misremembering things. I didn't fill these years with basketball at all. The last game I had watched was the Warriors game against the Trail Blazers when Curry performed magic. Basketball had to go. It smelled like America. A country where no one cared that I had been born, or where everyone I had ever known was mad at me or disappointed in me or worse.

I tried to forget everything about "home" and make a new one in the city where I had no close relations. I slipped deeper into my shell, that full body mask, a panzer no mirror could get past. Whenever I did look in the mirror, the only thing I saw was shame, the cruel joke of my name. Only a single letter away, my name has often been mistaken for shame or even sung to the tune of Shirley & Co.'s bygone hit: "Shame, shame, Shane, shame on you . . ." The shame was so overwhelming that now it is difficult to wade through its fog and reconstruct what came next. Perhaps there are things we forget that are better left in the unknown. Memory may only reactivate them, sticking them on repeat.

Then it was March 15, 2013. A Friday, on the date that would have been Grace and my five-year wedding anniversary. I went out to celebrate at a club called Chester's, where I met up with a group of people who didn't know I had been married. This didn't matter, because it wasn't what we were collectively celebrating. Like we did almost every night, this transient group of new Berliners and I were celebrating the sense of freedom that Berlin granted us. Having unchained ourselves from all the heavy relations of family and language and nation, we were untethered in a dirt-cheap metropolis, living it up. None of the people I was with that night spoke the native language of the country we were now living in, but it didn't matter—English was the lingua franca. And it didn't matter that I didn't know any of their names; there was no need to learn them. We'd all meet up at the same bar or club or gallery opening anyway and celebrate being far away from wherever home was.

That night, I made the mistake of mixing my recently prescribed antipsychotics with beer and ecstasy—something I hadn't taken since Grace proposed to me. Although I remember basically nothing from the evening, I do remember standing in line for the bathroom. I remember trying to walk through the bathroom door and being cut off by a large group of men and women. I remember closing my eyes and licking my teeth as the E started picking up and then opening my eyes when the door opened. I remember a hard-looking dude giving me a look. I remember him calling me a faggot as I uncontrollably licked my teeth from the E. I also remember smiling at him and asking, *Does your masculinity feel threatened or are you tempted?* Then I remember his hands wrapping around my neck.

When I came to the next day, there were two unfamiliar people in my apartment. I vaguely recognized them from O Tannenbaum, another bar I went to, but their faces looked different in the daylight. They looked worried. They asked me whether I could remember anything that had happened the night before at O Tannenbaum. I said that I didn't go to O Tannenbaum, I was at Chester's. They shook their heads in contradiction, then notified me that I had walked into O Tannenbaum alone in the early morning. I didn't say hello to anyone and went straight to the bathroom. When they heard a loud noise, they broke down the bathroom door. I was found on the floor with my belt around my neck. I had tried to hang myself from the pipes above the toilet. I had fallen, destroying the toilet and the mirror above the sink. It was quiet, which is why they had heard me.

At my insistence, they took me home instead of the hospital. Out of goodwill, they stayed with me to make sure I didn't do anything stupid. They asked me if I had anyone I could call who could look after me, then waited until someone I had dated came over. I was deeply ashamed as Regina took off the sheets and discovered that I had wet the bed.

I had to get away.

Friends from Berlin who had moved back to New York understood from my cryptic Gchats that I was in some sort of crisis. After I told them that I was walking around the house meowing like a cat, they begged me to come stay with them in that overly friendly way of Americans, often with people they hardly know. I distrusted the sincerity of such gestures—and even now I struggle to believe them—and wrote that I hadn't been back since I filed my divorce papers and that I didn't plan on returning. They begged some more, promising that they would make America fun again. At a loss of what I should be doing with myself, I booked the next available flight, I could almost afford it, then took time off from the bookstore, and tried to not regret my decision.

When I arrived in Bushwick two weeks after my suicide attempt, Sophia and Rachel were relieved to see me. I had stopped answering their emails and they weren't entirely sure if I was coming. I showered after the long journey and we talked for a while before they had to go to work. They told me to call them if I needed anything or wasn't feeling well and I said I already felt better; it was good to be away from Berlin. I almost meowed as a joke but didn't want to worry them. I thanked them instead.

Alone on their sofa, I picked up the book of poems lying on the coffee table. I flipped to the page that matched my birth year, something I always do, turning a book of poems into a Choose Your Own Adventure novel, a roulette wheel. The poem was titled "The Convalescent," an unappealing idea. I skipped ahead a hundred pages as per usual. I then read the following poem:

"Archaic Torso of Apollo"

We never knew his head and all the light
that ripened in his fabled eyes. But
his torso still burns like a streetlight dimmed
in which his gaze, lit long ago,

holds fast and shines. Otherwise the surge
of the breast could not blind you, nor a smile

run through the slight twist of the loins
toward that center where procreation flared.

Otherwise this stone would stand cut off
and cold under the shoulder's transparent drop
and not glisten like a wild beast's fur;

and not break forth from all its contours
like a star: for there is no place
that does not see you. You must change your life.

—translated by Edward Snow

I put down the copy of Rainer Maria Rilke's *New Poems*. I was terrified. I read the poem again and the last line felt like an indict-
ment. Rilke was right. I must change my life—but how? Without
guidelines, these oracular words were fireworks that burst and
no more. I looked for further assistance on the next page, in the
next poem, but it didn't offer any suggestion. Instead, it depicted
the huntress Artemis storming off in anger. I read the poem
about Apollo again and realized I was Apollo's torso, headless and
exposed. Then I read the poem about Artemis once more. Unsure
what it meant, I ate one of the bagels I had bought on my way
from the subway and took a nap.

For the next two weeks in New York, I walked around Manhattan
trying to memorize "Archaic Torso of Apollo" in German. I hoped
that the secret of how I could change my life would be released
if I could speak the words perfectly from memory. Day after day,

I failed on the seventh or ninth line, then took the train back to Brooklyn in the evenings where I met friends and friends of friends, poets all of them.

One night, I was supposed to meet Rachel for drinks in Williamsburg after she went to a reading. On my way out of the station, I walked by a sports bar and saw that the Warriors were playing the Denver Nuggets. I could tell by the lettering in the bottom right corner that it was the NBA playoffs. I was shocked. It seemed impossible that the Warriors were in the playoffs again—we were terrible. Weren't we? I entered the bar and texted Rachel to come.

To my great satisfaction, the bar was streaming the first game of the 2013 playoffs from the Warriors' feed on NBA League Pass, and I heard the familiar voices of the Warriors' announcers, Bob Fitzgerald and Jim Barnett. I smiled. Like in all those years I had watched the Warriors' broadcasts, I heard Barnett analyze the gameplay in his overly excited grandpa sort of way and the familiarity made me feel like a boy again. I could see all those years in front of the television and all the players I had loved in Oracle Arena: Chris Webber, Chris Mullin, Tim Hardaway, Mitch Richmond, Šarūnas Marčiulionis, Baron Davis, Latrell Sprewell. As I drifted into these warmer climes of my memory, my previous devotion to basketball appeared like an oasis.

Standing at the bar, I remembered the first time I went to Oracle, which was then called the Oakland–Alameda County Coliseum Arena. I remembered that my dad and I had seats in the nosebleeds and that I was very excited to be ditching school for basketball. I remembered being so enthralled and beside myself that I drooled on the t-shirt that my dad had bought me before the game, featuring cartoon caricatures of the team, and so there was a big pool of red slobber on Chris Mullin's head. I hadn't been paying enough attention while eating Hot Tamales and staring at the jumbotron. I remembered crying and my dad consoling me with the words, "Come on, this is awesome." The stadium was so loud and ebullient and it lifted my mood. And Oracle Arena would stay that way in all the years the Warriors were terrible. I also remembered that when we drove back home the next day, I picked up my ball and went onto our driveway that still had small piles of snow on it. There, I practiced Tim Hardaway's crossover, which I couldn't get quite right. I only went inside the house for dinner, my hands thoroughly frozen. It didn't matter.

As a child, basketball had meant the world to me. It provided a way to survive the daily domestic calamities, the occasional violence at home, and the boredom of the public school system. I would spend every afternoon after school in the fall and spring and all day during the summer shooting hoops on the rim above our garage door. With the length of happy days, I devised complicated games for myself, practiced the signature moves of star players, and invited neighborhood friends over to play on the driveway where I had home court advantage. I knew every crack in the asphalt, the gaps that approximated the three-point and free throw lines as well as where the ball would bounce out of alignment from the Ponderosa pine tree's carnage, the roots upheaving and destroying my kingdom. Such disastrous conditions were not irksome, just a given. Out on my court on Warr Road in South Lake Tahoe, California, nothing else mattered. I felt like a king.

Watching the Warriors lose to the Nuggets in the bar in

Williamsburg, I remembered that basketball had been almost alchemical when I was younger: it could change the color of the day, it could turn anger, fear, and boredom into—what was it exactly? Something better, something golden. I paused and remembered Rilke's final line. Then ordered another round for Rachel and me to say goodbye.

The next day, I flew back to the place I still call home and, like a true prodigal son, I threw myself into becoming reacquainted with my familiar territory. I stayed up all night in Berlin illegally streaming the first round of the playoffs, read about what I had missed in the three years where I didn't watch basketball. The Warriors had finally fired Don Nelson after that game against the Portland Trail Blazers and now everything was changing. They were becoming an actually decent team under Mark Jackson, perhaps even better than that. Feeling inspired, I decided to disobey my doctor, the man who had performed the surgery on my back. On my final obligatory checkup in June 2005, he had insisted that I could never play contact sports again: it was too risky and might damage his work, which he had admired as he ran his fingers up my naked spine like a sculptor. I had listened to him in all those years after, when I could no longer bend over to tie my shoes—the metal rods and the fused vertebrae made me unbendable. But back in Berlin and excited for the first time in years, I bought a ball and shot a lot of bricks for a couple of days, with the belief that basketball might change something, my love might bring me out of my misery. One evening, I dared to take part in a pickup game at Hasenheide park. In that first game, I made a backdoor cut and went up for an easy layup. I played alright for the rest of the game and was surprised to be invited to come play the next evening. I felt like a boy again.

But once I was alone again in my apartment, I felt like a mere manchild. I had left New York with that Rilke line buzzing in my head and the idea that perhaps basketball might be the key to a life without anxiety, without loneliness, as it had solved so many problems before. I hoped that basketball would help me to start living with a sense of purpose. Love is known to be all powerful. It is said to destroy all boundaries. But it was unable to get through the corset. I was still a mess whenever I was alone with myself.

I thought about letting it go. It was just a poem. A very good poem, yes, but definitely not a spell or a citation or an invoice—though it tormented me like all three of them combined.

You must change your life.

How? I wasn't about to turn to some stupid self-help manual. What I did instead was throw myself into basketball, which turned out to be a way to avoid myself. I spent countless days looking up statistics or watching old clips, seeing everything I had missed. I invested even more time in the Warriors, whose story was more promising. They were on an upward trajectory ever since the game I had watched against the Trail Blazers and things looked like they were going to get even better. We had the best backcourt in NBA history, Steph Curry and Klay Thompson were . . .

There was that nagging voice again.

You must change your life.

But what about—

You must change your life.

You must change your life.
You must change your life.
You must change your life!
Basketball was just a distraction.
Until it wasn't.

Toward the start of the 2015–16 season, I was scanning Reddit's r/warriors feed on my phone. There was a lot of buzz around the team since the new head coach, Steve Kerr, led the Warriors to our first championship in 40 years. Every sandwich, interaction, and opinion was recorded and distorted into something about greatness. The first article linked in the r/warriors feed was no different. It was from yesterday, November 27, 2015, and it made the obligatory passing mention about the Warriors winning the 2015 NBA championship and then detailed a pep talk Kerr gave to the team before the seventeenth game of the season.

At the time, Kerr was actually away from the daily life of the Warriors as he was nursing his back after a botched surgery, but the article suggested Kerr was something like the holy spirit guiding the Warriors to victory. He did this by establishing the team's four core values of joy, mindfulness, compassion, and competition, which would not only help them to be better players on the court but to also be better people off it.

It was like lightning.

My jaw dropped and I wanted to guffaw but then I had a flash of bounce passes. Of slapping hands after a good play and how people played together. The rude bruisers who inflict violence in pickup games like their lives depended on winning. The flashy movers who want to look nice above everything else. The me-first ball hogs in parks and gyms who always wonder why no one wanted to play with them. There are loud talkers in pickup games who call foul when no foul has been committed and quiet warriors who let their work speak for them. There are people who never want to get in the way and those who only came out to get some exercise and have a little fun. There are also the overambitious who try to do everything alone.

What turned some of the most famous relentless lone gunners into great basketball players was that they learned to trust their teammates. While continuing to deliver excellence, players like Michael Jordan and Kobe Bryant learned to relinquish absolute control and their trust turned them into champions. But then how did this change take place? I remembered that both Jordan and Bryant only started winning once they were coached by Phil Jackson, basketball's "Zen Master"—who had also been Steve Kerr's coach!

It was getting dramatic.

Was I getting this right?

Was Kerr suggesting turning his four core values into a life practice?

And: if you can change your habits on the court, can you shift that wisdom off it?

Suddenly I had the light inside and everything was visible.

I would change my life.

By living according to the Warriors four core values: joy, mindfulness, compassion, and competition.

This is how I entered the paradox: letting go of what I knew before and saying yes to everything that was new and unfamiliar, while also having a distaste for self-improvement—a very neoliberal undertaking, but one that also seemed necessary. Not only because I had seen where my distrust of the world had led me—a belt and a bathroom with weak PVC pipes—but also because I had started a new relationship and I didn't want it to end with unspoken truths or unsent emails. I had been in a few relationships since Grace and they always ended badly because I wasn't ready to look at myself. Now, I wanted to.

Melanie and I had met at an introductory reception in mid-June 2015, shortly after the Warriors won their first championship. We had both been hired as "interpreters" of one of her brother's pieces at a retrospective of his work at the Martin Gropius Bau. That afternoon, the twenty-odd interpreters of the piece stood in a large circle and introduced themselves. One accomplished academic after another tooted their horn, and by the seventh one I started feeling like they had made a mistake casting me—I was only a bookseller who had written and translated a few things here and there. Standing to my left was Melanie. "Hi, my name's Melanie, I'm Tino's little sister, so I have to be here. I'm a professor of sorts at Frankfurt Oder and I work on Alfred North Whitehead, William James, and Donna Haraway," she said by way of introduction, and I was in love. She was absolutely beautiful and she was humble. And she was working on the three philosophers who interested me and the poets I love the most. Not that I understood them, but I wanted to.

So, given this concatenation, I approached Melanie after we left the reception. The whole group was headed to a bar around the corner and I thought of something quick to make a good impression after my uninspired introduction to the group: "Hi, uhh, I'm Shane, I sell books and sometimes I work on them." Out on Stresemannstraße, I said out of nowhere: *Whatever is going to happen is already happening.*

I stood on the street and waited for a reaction from Melanie. But she just looked at me like I was a freak. I said, *That's Ted Berrigan.* And I knew that Berrigan had been very influenced by Whitehead when writing his *Sonnets. But,* I said, *that's actually Whitehead, isn't it?* She threw another confused look at me. I thought you just said it was Ted Berrigan, she said. I blushed. I had already messed this up. I tried to explain, was unable to. Then she made some joke I can no longer remember but I do remember thinking that this was absolutely terrible—she was witty, slightly nerdy, but totally down to earth. My God! I had seen enough gangster movies to know that you should never get too familiar with your boss' sister, things were always bound to end in disaster. It was for this reason that, when we arrived at the bar, I asked the coordinators of the piece, Louise and Descha, to never allow me to work with Melanie. I was too scared of making a fool of myself in front of her, or, even worse, demonstrating my newfound adoration.

And we didn't work together. We only connected at the closing party for the show in mid-August, and from there entered a cautious and awkward start of our relationship. I decided to be as honest as possible so that we would not have any nasty surprises later. I told her about the suicide attempt, the back surgery, the previous marriage, and I told her even more. I told her about my homeless, unstable mother, my absent father, the favorite uncle who killed himself, my sister with panic attacks, the abuse as a child, the problems with alcohol, the student loan debt, the needing a way out. All those things I had been silent about for so many years.

Melanie listened to me. Then told me about her own fears and disappointments and problems. She told me about the squat she had lived in for eleven years near the pool I swam at and what she had learned about the difficult necessity of community. She told me about her meditation practice and her work, which was focused on the decolonization of our minds while never denying the advances of science. We went on long walks through Schöneberg, where Melanie lived, and in Gleisdreieckpark, and talked and talked in the rain. None of this was romantic, but for us it was necessary. It was also often very funny.

During October and November 2015, we started building a bond where we could find strength in one another—or, as the Warriors say, where we could find our "Strength in Numbers." Where we could encourage one another to start over whenever we were overwhelmed and felt like giving up. (But then, I was really the only one who felt like giving up; Melanie was much further in her development.) Whenever I lost sight of the goals that I set myself. Which I often did because I couldn't forget backward, couldn't always outrun the past. I had all these bad habits like beer and cigarettes and distrust of others. But she would console me with the idea that I was just starting a process of becoming. She encouraged me with a lot of the words that I recognized from Steve Kerr. When I told her about the four core values on one of our long walks in Gleisdreieckpark in late November, she encouraged me to follow the Warriors' example. She had to endorse this journey of learning through experience: she is a pragmatist, after all.

And so, I decided I would. I would change my life—and Melanie and Coach Kerr would help me. Love would not change me on its own, but it would give me the courage to make the effort and the goal to strive toward. None of this would be linear or definite after the first rational acquisition but it would slowly become all encompassing. Nothing could go untouched if I was to be serious about joy, mindfulness, compassion, and competition. It would mean reaching out to my estranged family and taking care of my estranged friends and even my enemies. It would mean being engaged and finding myself more in relation to the world. By conjuring up countless other voices and engaging with my surroundings as much as possible, following the Warriors's values would also mean going beyond the self of the neoliberal *self*-improvement. It would mean at times even dropping the self and being left with the improvement. And then dropping improvement as well. We don't need it. We all have the light inside and it's only a question of finding what is already there.

All of this would mean learning as much as unlearning—and forgetting. Learning new ways of being and unlearning the entrenched mechanisms and procedures that kept me attached to what I no longer wanted. Above all, it would mean learning to stick with it, even if the game lasts much longer than you expected.

What you have in your hands is a document of my attempt to change my life. The book may go very far afield from this simple statement, but then we cannot settle for *too much* oversimplification if we want to do justice to the complex relations of the clusterfuck called the world.

And so, here we are, the players, in the world.

There's no one on the bench and we're down by ten but there's still some time on the clock.

Let's make magic together.

Joy

ON FAMILY, HOMELESSNESS, LUCK, AND THE
GREATNESS OF STEPHEN CURRY
June 23, 2016

My sister's getting the health care she needs and my mother's no longer living on the streets.

Bitte? Please?

Excuse me, I know. That could have been more graceful. It could have used some padding between the clauses, some form of explanation. But as I sat on a park bench on Fasanenplatz just days after the Warriors lost to the Cleveland Cavaliers in the 2016 NBA Finals, I was oblivious to any incredulity, except, of course, I wasn't. The elder German woman sitting next to me had asked about my family, hadn't she? And I had tried to explain the changes America was undergoing with experiences I knew, right? It wasn't my intention to shock her. Like I said, I was happy. I was happy my family was receiving the services they needed. I did say I was happy, didn't I? Excuse me, I . . .

After this outburst though, the elder German woman didn't want to hear any more. She was staring at me as if I were a madman. Then she looked around the small cobbled square to make sure others were in earshot and picked up her newspaper. There was a light breeze. Light was streaming through the linden trees. I pulled out a cigarette. I was totally flustered. The conversation I had just ruined had begun innocently enough.

I had mentioned that Melanie and I were thinking of moving in together and that we were looking at an apartment tomorrow in the neighborhood. I had also said I wanted to get a feel for the area first and visit the house Brecht had lived in before his years of exile, which was around the corner—but this was only a half-truth. The house had been bombed out and the real reason I was there was because I didn't want to sit around my apartment re-watching the final devastating moments of Game 7. I was still haunted by Curry's foolish behind the back pass that went out of bounds, the spectacular chase down block on Andre Iguodala's layup attempt by the Cleveland Cavaliers' LeBron James, and Kyrie Irving's game- and series-winning three over Curry's outstretched arms, which meant that we lost the Finals after being up 3–1 and had ruined a perfect season, where we had more wins than any other team in NBA history (73).

The elder German woman snapped me out of my negative reveries. She said that she thought that our looking for a place was *schön* but then wondered about my family in America. Didn't I miss them? The country was in a downward spiral, *oder?* I told her it was complicated.

Then I unloaded the first sentence of this chapter. She must have found it hard to believe that my mother had been homeless given what she assumed to be my status, affirmed by my clothing and capability in German. That or she thought I was a terrible son. How could I let my mom wander the streets alone when I was obviously in a better position? Was the elder German woman judging me? Or was I judging me? As I exhaled the smoke, she got up to leave. *Auf Wiedersehen. Tschüß.*

On the bench alone I asked myself: what could be more depressing? That the elder German woman didn't seem to believe me? Or that happiness and luck are practically indistinguishable? You don't believe me? Look it up in the dictionary.

While used differently, *Glück*, which was the word that had been hovering over both of our heads, means both happiness and luck. This isn't some German perversion. The cognate for happiness is "luck" in every Indo-European language. The *heur* in *bonheur* is salvaged from the Old French for luck, and English happiness comes from the Old Norse *hap* for—you guessed it— luck. Chaucer: *"Thus kan Fortune hir wheel governe and gye, / And out of joye brynge men to sorwe."* Translation: our happenstance and hence our happiness are dictated by the wheel of fortune. We forfeit our joy, which is only an extreme form of happiness, to the casino floor, to the roulette wheel or craps table, and that inalienable right of the U.S. Constitution to pursue happiness has bad odds, high stakes, and payment in steak dinners at a restaurant you'd never want to eat at anyway. *Please?*

Modern English has made its Old Norse origins subterranean in comparison to German's birch-like surface roots snaking along the mossy floor of the forest, yet we still live as if happiness is conditional in English, as if it hinges on whatever follows the relative pronoun or preposition: I am happy *that* _____ or, I am happy *for* _____, etc. And long before I tried to express my happiness to the elder German woman on a warm afternoon not long after the Warriors were extremely unlucky, I had learned to believe that joy was nothing more than a category of snapshots to be bought from Shutterstock or a morsel sold with a jingle. Although both subscribed to effervescent forms of happiness, this belief didn't come from my culture or upbringing. It sprung from my studies of "the most noble discipline," where I learned that philosophy's principle goal is to learn how to perish. My cumbersome, life-sapping student debt may be testament to my investment in this pursuit, but I confess I never found a compelling answer to this fundamental question in analytic philosophy's acrobatics of necessary and sufficient conditions for things as simple as walking to the bathroom.

More discouraging than investing years in the baroque rabbit holes of modal logic and JTB+ (don't look it up) was that analytic philosophy never offered any alternatives to them, and insisted that once we die, we're only dust and bones. If living meant being busy with such loveless schemes in preparation for a death that was final and without reward, I began to wonder: where did we go wrong? Shouldn't we prepare ourselves to die by living? And: whatever happened to happiness? Was it clear cut for something more sinister? Bovines and soybeans? Speculation? I thought this was a protected forest!

It wasn't. We cleared it away. When? Sometime after Aristotle said, "Happiness is a life lived according to virtue." Now we dodge between the stumps of Theodor Adorno's "There is no right life in the wrong" and forage for gobs of luck. Even worse: if Adorno was right, then it had never been any better. Slavery permeated every ancient culture and the American Dream was the privilege of slaveholders.

This train of thought ended and I got up from the bench and decided to go home since I didn't have to go to work. As I unlocked my bike to return to Neukölln, I wondered whether happiness needed different tactics. Perhaps happiness needs to be approached like a battle. Maybe we should go to war with what oppresses us—maybe we need to fight what bars the door to fulfilment and pleasure. But how many survive such a mutiny? And how many survivors require medication after the trauma of warfare? Could it be that Aristotle was right? That happiness is not rebellious, only mundane? Does that take luck to find?

Back at my apartment, I picked up one of the books of poems lying on my bed and flipped to my birth year. It was the second half of a poem, so I went to page 81 in my Faber and Faber edition of *The Complete Poems* of Emily Dickinson. I found this:

'Tis so much joy! 'Tis so much joy!
If I should fail, what poverty!
And yet, as poor as I
Have ventured all upon a throw;
Have gained! Yes! Hesitated so –
This side the victory!

Life is but Life! And Death, but Death!
Bliss is, but Bliss, and Breath but Breath!
And if I indeed fail,
At least, to know the worst, is sweet!
Defeat means nothing but Defeat,
No drearier, can befall!

And if I gain! Oh Gun at Sea!
Oh Bells, that in the Steeples be!

At first, repeat it slow!
For Heaven is a different thing,
Conjectured, and waked sudden in –
And might extinguish me!

What luck! This was great! But wait! What about that stutter step in the definition of bliss, which seems to be infected with desperation? Then there's the end, which seems to be no better than Chaucer's wheel of fortune. Heaven might not only *brynge* me to *sorwe*, it might also destroy me! I was back at contingency. And gloom. I felt very near what I was trying to leave. It gave me the creeps.

I opened my browser and opened the saved bookmark, like I did every time that I felt miserable and wanted to give up. I then read the article that would start my journey.

Sidelined from his team's historic start to the 2015–16 season by a botched back surgery after herniating a disk celebrating the Warriors' 2015 NBA championship, Steve Kerr visited the Golden State Warriors' practice facility in November 2015 to talk to the team about the state of things. The Warriors had just won sixteen games in a row and Kerr was proud of their performance in his absence. Not because they were winning, which was great, of course, but because they were executing according to his four core values. As I read this article again, I noted that, in his reported speech, Kerr placed emphasis on joy.

Kerr wants his team to play with joy, he wants them to be happy. He wants them to have fun and enjoy what they're doing. Not only because they're privileged to be earning more money yearly than the average American will in a lifetime—which they are—but because they are able to do what they love and they should love what they do; both on and off the court.

This is something that Stephen Curry, the leader of the team, has seemed to embody from the beginning. Curry makes the impression of being a happy-go-lucky person who also enjoys being mischievous. His child-like silliness is often expressed during pre-game warmup routines where he acts like a bowling pin. With his arms crossed across his chest, he marvels at the ball slowly rolling toward his feet while his teammates prepare for the challenge of the game ahead. Eyes wide and jaw dropped, Curry pretend faints when the ball grazes his feet then stands up and performs a 360 in the air before crouching and launching the ball into the basket.

The merriment of the Baby-Faced Assassin carries into the game itself when he passes the ball to Draymond Green at the top of the key, then curls around a screen at the baseline, shooting a three and galloping down the court like an overexcited foal prancing in an open field. Over the years, Curry has developed a large repertoire of awkward celebrations. There's the can-can kicks of line dancers, the dad-like "raising the roof," or the shoulder shimmy out of the Roaring Twenties. Most famously, Curry is known for his turnaround threes, where he doesn't even bother to see whether the ball has achieved its goal. As the greatest shooter to ever play the game, he doesn't need to. Statistically, he has the effective field goal rate of highly efficient centers and what is remarkable about this statistical feat is that Curry does not take most of his shots close to the basket like these highly efficient and *tall* centers. Instead, he'll pull up from thirty feet, further from the basket than anyone who came before him, then chew on the mouth guard that's hanging out of his mouth after the ball goes through the net, a totally un-macho gesture that makes him look like a teenager.

Curry's reckless delight can also be documented in countless highlights where he lets his ebullience get the better of him. The most heartbreaking example of his looseness was a few days before I talked to the elder German woman, during Game 7 of the 2016 Finals, when he attempted a behind the back pass to Klay Thompson halfway through the fourth quarter. While the ball sailed out of bounds, even Curry knew this turnover was completely unnecessary. The Warriors were clinging to a one-point lead and a simple pass would have perfectly served the purpose. But then, as the saying goes: "Steph's gonna Steph."

Sitting at home and trying to reconnect with the value of joy, I remembered that I experienced a new height of the Warriors' embodiment of the value when Curry "ventured upon a throw" a half-court heave against the Oklahoma City Thunder to win in overtime on February 27, 2016. When the ball went through the net, I was ecstatic. The team was ecstatic. Even opposing and bandwagon Warriors fans in attendance in Oklahoma City were ecstatic. We had all just witnessed something incredible. So incredible, in fact, that it's worth a closer look.

With the game tied at 118 in overtime, the Thunder's Russell Westbrook misses a contested shot and the Warriors' Andre Iguodala secures the rebound. There are 6.8 seconds on the clock and Iguodala passes the ball to Curry. Curry, almost casually, brings the ball to the half-court line then enters his shooting motion out of nowhere. With two steps, he crouches and shoots a shot defying all conventional wisdom. He is wide open, yes, but no one shoots from that distance with that much time on the clock (3.4 seconds). No one "settles" for such a shot when your team still has a timeout remaining, like the Warriors did. A heave like this is reserved for the final tenths of a second. This was why the Thunder defender, Andre Roberson, was not there to block Curry's shot. Roberson was wisely hovering around the three-point line where it could be expected Curry would approach and shoot from—that is, if the Warriors didn't call a timeout. The problem is that Curry has changed the dimensions of the game and weaponized a shot that had previously only been fit for games of H-O-R-S-E, forcing us to redefine our ideas about shot selection and solid defense. His release is so quick and his aim is so accurate that, statistically, a contested deep three is a layup for him.

And this shot certainly looked as easy as a lay-in. When the ball went through the net and the announcer Mike Breen exclaimed *"BANG! BANG! OH, WHAT A SHOT FROM CURRY,"* Curry broke the record for the most threes in a single game, as well as his own record for most threes made in a season with another month and a half remaining. (In the end, Curry would break the record for the most three-point field goals made in a season on three separate seasons: 272 in 2012–13; 286 in 2014–15; and then, in 2015–16, the same year he was the league's first-ever unanimous MVP, obliterating his own record with 402. In this season, now over after the heartbreaking loss to the Cavs, Curry would even come to be known in Mandarin as the "Skyfucker.")

While Curry danced and the rest of the team celebrated winning the game in Oklahoma City, I was covering my mouth, trying to not wake up my neighbors in my apartment building in Neukölln at 3:30 in the morning. I ripped my earbuds from my ears and I couldn't help it—I let out a little yell. I couldn't believe it. I was insanely happy and not only because my childhood team had finally pulled out of the decades of doldrums for good. They were doing something incredible and they were having a lot of fun doing it. Game after game, we all kept cycling through joy together. It was like cicadas waking up in the forest after years of staying subterranean, dormant. I realized now that this joy was even more than a preposition or conjunction. I realized what Donna Haraway, the feminist theorist and daughter of a sportswriter, meant when she said joy is the "eternal suspension of time, a high of 'getting it' together in action."

Which is where we reach the chicken *and* the egg. Some might say the Warriors wouldn't be happy if they hadn't won the championship the season before. They might say that joy is dependent on victory. Such an interpretation won't do. The value of joy had been instated the day Kerr became the head coach of the team, and as the brief Curry interlude suggests, their star player had always approached the game with the same verve as a child. Instead, this situation is like what William James said. There are "cases where a fact cannot come at all unless a preliminary faith exists in its coming." If we learned to live as if joy were already present and not contingent on success, then the weird thing is that the championship, the ring, is more likely to come. As the Warriors teach, the trophy is yours if you learn to have fun in the daily grind. If and when it comes, your happiness will only be briefly increased by the trophy. Joy cannot be dependent on results. It must be its own reward. The one catch is you can't trick yourself. You can't pretend to believe. You actually have to believe. You have to scream "WE BELIEVE," just like the 2006–07 Warriors did. It's so simple, insane even, and it actually works. This doesn't mean that everything will work to your advantage through belief alone. It needs hard work, too. Even then you might fail, as the Warriors have shown. Still, joy is the first, most crucial step. And this seems applicable off the court as well.

At the same time I was following the start of the 2015–16 NBA season and beginning my relationship with Melanie, my mother was finalizing the paperwork for her third attempt at a disability claim. She had been denied twice before for very questionable reasons, yet she never gave up. During the months of October, November, and December 2015, she followed up with the doctors and psychologists in San Luis Obispo, delivered their reports to pro bono lawyers, and was early for every court appearance. She had high spirits whenever we talked, although she was living in a homeless shelter. She would report about her daily comings and goings and we had finally developed some rapport after a decade of estrangement—something Melanie encouraged me to do. Previously, I had been enraged or disengaged on those rare occasions we spoke, reserved for holidays or emergencies. I would try to give advice about finding an apartment, a job, or maintaining friendships but these finer details got lost in our battles about accountability, about who ruined whom and how they weren't sorry but would be. There was often rage in her voice as well as desperation. There was also an occasional slur. When that happened, her threats to commit suicide were just threats as often as not. When they weren't and she survived, I became acquainted with a whole new vocabulary of hospitals and law enforcement.

There was the 5150, the NFA, the BOP, and their consequences. There were dropped charges and storage units and new numbers. There were the years of absolute silence after my divorce. The last time I saw my mother before I spoke to the elder German woman in June 2016 was when I flew to California to sign my divorce papers and visited her on Christmas Day. She was drunk and alone in my grandmother's house in South Lake Tahoe, where she was living at the time. She was going on at length about how everyone had abandoned her except me and that she had repaid the favor by taking care of me in the hospital after my spinal fusion in 2005.

That day, she told me about something I had forgotten. The catheter band had slipped below my knee and yanked on my urethra when I was unconscious and in obvious discomfort. She commended herself for realizing my distress and mending the situation. She mentioned that she had held my grown penis in her hands, which she described in detail. She then said I was the only good man in her life before trying to kiss me with her tongue. I left, immediately, with my mother's tongue imprint on my cheek. I later heard that she had fallen down the stairs, into the snow, and was found by the neighbors, near hypothermia I was told.

She didn't stay there very long. She kept moving. For years, I never bothered to write down the address of where she was staying because an envelope with a small amount of money would never arrive in time. She'd already be gone. To the next town where no one could harass her. To the next place, away from some malignant family member. To some mythical land where she could start all over.

As my mom's physical mobility declined, she experienced a heightened sense of liberty in San Luis Obispo in 2015. Her back problems—which are inoperable, unlike mine or Steve Kerr's—caused her a lot of pain, yet she was no longer asking for a handout, a divine retribution for the numerous injustices she had experienced at the hands of men. The assuredly justified rage inside her had subsided. It had proven itself to be a bad strategy, a cycling through of repetitive feelings. What was done was done, but what *could* be done—now that was exciting! She could help others without a known residence get off the bottle by listening to them. She could talk to the librarian about crystals to receive more reading material about healing. She could listen to the shelter's acclaimed street preacher and see scripture from the eyes of people she could identify with. She could help with the distribution of meals as well as get to know the volunteers when receiving her pain medication. She could walk in the sun in November and smile. She could eternally suspend time, in action.

One morning, in December 2015, she was on the way to her social worker. I called her as she was getting on the bus and she greeted a couple of people. It sounds like you've got a lot of friends, I said.

And some enemies, she said, but whatever.

She laughed. I laughed as well. I tried to picture who these enemies were, whether they were the ones she had greeted. It was then that I noticed my mother had become much happier since she was definitively homeless. Sure, she hadn't had her own apartment or a bank account for a decade, but she had almost always stayed with family members and entered a complicated economics of gratitude and obligation; a mental reckoning of indebtedness tallied out in beds and groceries and accusations. As the eldest daughter who had been continuously raped by her father, my mother felt entitled to receive assistance from her mother and two younger sisters who had always been aware of his transgressions. She also felt entitled to receive occasional payment from my father after he had lowballed her during their divorce proceedings. When he lost basically everything during the financial crisis, she reconsidered. She reconsidered accepting my offers to help her get off the streets as well and denied my attempts to fly her over to Germany. She asked for only one thing: love.

Now on the streets for an extended period of time, she was changing. It would be foolish to believe this cheer had anything to do with luck. Her luck couldn't have been any worse. At the bottom of society, she had lost everything, repeatedly, and had found something more valuable.

If this is luck, it is the luck of discovering what was already there. That rage toward the past only clouds the present and disallows a better future. Some might object that they know this from somewhere. It's a cliché, they'll say. It's in some film. Maybe it is. Maybe once you lose it all you realize there was nothing much to lose. Or maybe—and I find this much more compelling—she had learned that everything depends on your attitude and that your attitude doesn't mean forgetting. It just means changing your perspective. Our family motto, inherited from our Georgian Molokan ancestors (an Eastern Orthodox sect that was thoroughly defiant to authority figures), has always been: "The only person you can change is yourself." It was our secret family wisdom that none of us bothered to listen to.

Out on the streets of San Luis Obispo, my mom seemed to be finally getting it. Instead of seeing life as a challenge, even though it was challenging, she laughed as she went from homeless shelter to library to social worker to doctor to library to lawyer to church to shelter. She was doing something. The only thing I hate is boredom, she once told me. That seemed right. My mom was relearning what every child already knows: joy is not a noun. It's in the verb. And I was relearning that with and from her, and from Coach Kerr as well.

As Kerr stated in an interview with the Positive Coaching Alliance, "We're all in the development business." And it's a business that's always in need of repairs. In the time between writing this and my conversation with the elder German woman on the park bench on Fasanenplatz, my mom has lost the roof over her head. She is homeless again. She's spending time at a shelter in Chico, California, but she hasn't lost her determination. For a while, she had tried to help my sister. They had lived together in Portland, Oregon, in the first half of 2016 to get my sister to come to terms with her panic disorder. It didn't work. For multiple reasons. But like a DJ, I'd rather jump to the next track and not let this one crash.

Cue up our old Georgian wisdom.

Cue up the will to believe.

My mom is lucky to finally receive social security and to have the chance to get on some housing listings in a culture that doesn't see shelter as an inalienable right, and I am happy that she won't always have to walk on the streets all day in pain. This is what I would have wanted to tell the elder German woman on the park bench. None of that has changed even though my mom is homeless once again. I hope my mom's situation will soon change for the better but there are no guarantees. It will take some work. Some luck, too.

Something which Melanie and I will definitely need as well. It was looking like it would be pretty difficult to find an apartment in Berlin. We didn't even bother viewing the apartment around the corner from Fasanenplatz because there were dozens of people waiting for the real estate agent to arrive outside the main door. It was depressing. When I told my mom what had happened, she told me to buck up. I said I was trying. She asked me about my pledge to live according to the Warriors' four core values and I said I was trying to do that, too. Whereupon she answered, "Not to get all Yoda on you, but there is no try, *do*."

Beginning, Again

ON ORACLES AND SELF-HELP

But how do you do?

You consult an oracle. You make offerings. Gold and silver, pottery. Then you slaughter whatever there is to slaughter, you make sacrifices. In Delphi, to Apollo. Once you've completed all the warm-up routines in front of the temple, you then read the three maxims—Know Thyself, Nothing to Excess, and Surety Brings Ruin—and get ready to receive the message.

Afterward, you spend your days unraveling the riddles the Pythia relayed. If the oracle's pronouncement about your future is unambiguous, this doesn't mean that the pronouncement's meaning and application won't be. Just like when the Oracle of Delphi explained to Croesus, the king of Lydia, that a great empire would fall if he attacked Persia. He attacked Persia and the Pythia was right: an empire crumbled, Croesus' own. He had allowed himself to be tempted, he heard what he wanted to hear and not what she had said. Croesus had no one to blame for his failure but himself.

And so, what do you do after that?

Even if the stakes weren't as high as with Croesus, you still might feel like you've ruined your life. The life that you have tried to change through the advice from outside sources, through self-help manuals that also speak in Pythian riddles. What do you do after you fail to embody the tightly packed aphorisms that you have highlighted or underlined on their sleek pages? Do you blame eating a piece of cake on a bad day or do you condemn the whole system of dieting? Maybe you make self-accusations when you don't throw away a pack of cigarettes. You were told to feel pity for smokers huddling under entryways on cold and rainy days in the book that guaranteed you would never smoke again once you finished reading it, but in fact you feel envy. You also feel like a failure so you might as well enjoy yourself in this failure. As you inhale the smoke from the first cigarette from a fresh pack, it is clear to you that you have learned nothing from the book's contents.

So, what do you do?

You blame yourself, you curse your fate. You make comparisons. Everyone else, the baker, the grocer, your friends, your neighbor, they are all in control of their lives, of their destinies, and it is only you who is so lost as to require the guidance of an astrologer, a Tarot reading. This is a rather twisted form of narcissism, but it is mine. I am special because I am broken.

Then you realize all advice contains a lie. It makes life a straight line and denies any swerving. The times when you don't want to do anything but sleep until late in the afternoon or drink a whole bottle of wine and not listen to some successful person mythologize their rise to stardom, their justifications for why they deserve their riches. Advice forgets that some things are not possible, and that success isn't guaranteed if you listen. Advice hides the fact that sometimes you are lucky and that sometimes it is better to be lucky than to be good. Advice would be embarrassed to admit that it is a lot easier to be rich if you start rich and it would definitely deny that progress is not everything. Worst of all, advice also makes you feel like you are worse than you already are.

But what do you do when you know the Oracle is right? When you feel, deep down, that you would like to change your life? That you are in danger of forgetting the best version of yourself that you agreed to strive toward?

You try to stop comparing your life to others. If you haven't caused irreparable damage, you repair whatever is broken. You throw out the manuals that only reinforce a negative self-image, and you start again. And then you start again when that time didn't work out either. You start again and you start again. You keep starting until you die. It might be the only way to keep living and not just continue slowly dying.

Mindfulness

ON WORK, CIGARETTES, PREPPERS, AND BEING
IN THE ZONE WITH KLAY THOMPSON
November 13, 2017

Let's say you were right. If you lasered your eyes, your life would be better. You would no longer stumble through entrances and rooms when your lenses fogged up in winter and there would be no awkward encounters at the pool when you mistook someone for another. You said it again. If you had the cash, you'd fix your astigmatism. Then you'd buy supplies, a generator, and a gun, as well as some property in Brandenburg, away from the coast and the city. With your new eyes, you would be able to read the amount of protein on a can of your stockpiled chili without squinting, and you'd never be distracted by reflections whenever you emptied cartridges into a silhouette at the range on the weekend. You'd even consider getting a dog, for companionship and protection. At night and in the forest, full of wild boars and nocturnal marauders, another set of optics would be crucial.

As you licked your glasses and rubbed the lenses on your dress shirt, an emergency protocol set off within me, little bells and flashing imagery. Before this apocalyptic vision, I had wanted to suggest that the Warriors' understanding of mindfulness might help you get over your paranoid fantasies, like it was starting to help me with smoking and a bunch of other things, but now I didn't know how to introduce the subject. Were you really gaining experience with weapons? The specificity was telling. It felt like an annoyance that could only come from repetition, at a shooting range—where? Here in Berlin? I looked into your dark eyes and became worried, but this worry got stuck in my shoulders. They were tightening with negative energy.

That and I needed a cigarette. No. I didn't. Stop it. I needed to breathe. Breathe. I did. As I simulated the warm sensation of inhaling smoke at my place of work, St. George's Bookshop in Prenzlauer Berg, the emergency beacon's redness strobed slower inside me. I turned my head, right then left, then rotated my wrist to release the tension in my elbow.

I played stupid.

If doomsday did come and you survived, I asked, wouldn't your vision be clouded over by the implications? I mean, wouldn't it be wrong for the rich to survive just because of their money? Whatever, you said, quoting Brecht, *erst kommt das Fressen, dann kommt die Moral*. You smiled wryly. You knew that I originally came to Berlin to study Brecht and were now using it against me. I gave a fake laugh and rearranged some books on the reserve shelf behind me at the counter. It was a sleight of hand, a distraction from my real motivation, to breathe again, deeper and with purpose. Which worked for about two and a half seconds. I needed a cigarette and you were accusing me of something—that was clear through the withdrawal's irritability—since this tidbit fit into our past arguments.

I remembered how you, breathe in, had once come into the

bookstore and sworn allegiance to a group of activists in Hamburg who had dressed up as superheroes and who then shoplifted expensive foodstuffs from an upscale supermarket and redistributed the goods to the homeless at the train station. Breathe out. I remembered how I said this sounds more like a publicity stunt than activism, breathe in, and how you said, *Exactly, we need to broadcast inequality.* Breathe out. You then quoted these same words of Brecht after I said it was pointless, breathe in, and maybe even immoral to put the homeless in a position of having to explain themselves to the authority figures for the crémant, caviar, and beef tartar at their disposal. Breathe out. It was presumptuous to believe the recipients would even eat it— my mother, for one, hates caviar. And how often is unwanted food thrown away by panhandlers? Breathe in. You can only eat so many *belegte Brötchen* in a day and maybe you don't like salami or hardboiled eggs. Breathe out. And maybe you want a bottle of water or beer and not the patronizing gesture of some supposedly good-natured citizen who gives you bread instead of money so that you don't quote spend it on alcohol or drugs end quote. Breathe in. As if you have any right to act paternally and not like a sister or brother! Breathe out. What we need is the warmth of a smile! A cigarette! True generosity! Without averting your eyes! Look closer! Breathe in! We are human!

The craving was passing. My breath was getting longer, my ribcage disentangled. But the lamb's wool inside my boots had dampened. This change in foot mugginess was nothing new. My toes had also sweat on Day Two and Day Three after quitting smoking and I had brought an extra pair of socks in my backpack for exactly this predicament. I didn't want to change them right now, though. I'd have to explain what I was going through, which I was ashamed of, and the store was too full to leave the counter to go to the bathroom. I sat down in the tall swivel chair again, adjusted my glasses and tuned in to your narration.

Außerdem, it would be your intelligence and planning that would ensure your survival, not your money, and it would be your right, if not your duty, to do so. Easy, I said, easy. I gestured toward the German History shelf. Another customer came to the counter. You folded your arms in like a beach chair, reluctantly moving over. I typed in the books' authors, titles, and prices into the spreadsheet: Morrison, *Beloved*, 6.50, Adichie, *Americanah*, 6, Butler, *Kindred*, 7.50. As I performed my duties, I couldn't tell whether my coded suggestion had made an impression. You were dismissively reading the back matter of the Invisible Committee's most recent publication, *Now*, that was on display to the right of the faux-mahogany counter, my only exit. I thought that this title might help introduce the Warriors and mindfulness but you snickered at what you were reading. I completed the transaction. Then my curiosity piqued. Do you really think you'd be ready for the apocalypse?

I mean, even if you had prepared everything at home, you still couldn't plan for what would be outside your door. There might be collapsed buildings, fires in the streets, pandemonium. You'd have to somehow reach your property in the country-side, hope that the roads still existed and weren't overrun with checkpoints, robbers. Who's to say your cellar wouldn't already be raided? These are a lot of big ifs you can't control, I said, so why not stop dreaming up fantasies of escape and stick with the present.

Now was my chance to insert the Warriors' understanding of mindfulness—but you cut me off.

It's inevitable, you said, like the four seasons.

Historical information would suggest we are entering society's hibernal (you actually used the word hibernal) and it only makes sense to prepare for the coming darkness. The 2008 financial crisis was only a dip into winter's destruction, the first taste of the subarctic austerity to come. You didn't seem upset about this. You were like a waiter reporting that not all dishes on the menu were available. And, you said, in your strange accent that had a British inflection although you mostly retained the informal lexicon of your native American, this shit will last much longer than projected.

Where were you getting all this?

You became interested in this "eventuality" when you bought the *SAS New and Updated Survival Handbook* by John "Lofty" Wiseman at a shop in London, used but in mint condition, where you learned that self-preservation is a force more powerful than a jet engine, as well as technical information about skinning a reindeer. Then you started watching the National Geographic Channel's *Doomsday Preppers*. At first you seesawed between laughing at the protagonists—whose improbable scenarios and medieval fears about solar blasts, market crashes, and volcanoes could easily be traced to their professional traumas as insurance salesmen, firefighters, and law enforcement—and being worried about their negative portrayals of human nature in times of crisis. Everyone was convinced of the next person's evil and they were only interested in themselves or their next of kin. Prepping seemed to be a perfect reflection of the morality of the market, the selfishness.

I guess it's also just giving in to fear, I said. To dread The End is human, but to prepare for the Second Coming with gas masks was irrational, impulsive. If these people confronted their anxiety, they wouldn't need any flamethrowers. I made a move to talk about the Warriors and presence but again you interjected.

I used to think that way too, you said. Then you reconsidered your dismissal of preppers when you read a *New Yorker* article in January 2017 about Silicon Valley's plans for the apocalypse. If the very people who believe, almost painfully, in the possibility of building a better future through technology have initiated plans of moving far away from fault lines, nuclear winds, and civilization to places like the southern island of New Zealand, then it was time to reconsider your future. You felt naïve and deceived as you read this article. The techies were like preppers but they seemed to know something about our current reality, where it was headed. When you later read a *Guardian* article about these technological pioneers weaning themselves and their children from the devices they had invented, you even began to seethe.

It was then that you decided to investigate your way of living. You wrote down everything you did in a day and spent a week unraveling each activity's operating systems. You were terrified by your dependence on the internet and satellites and logistics, on your slavery to electricity and to those who produce it, the sketchy nations and conglomerates. Even the water supply network is automated, you said, growing unexpectedly impatient. What would happen if all this went down? If the systems were hacked, intentionally, to create chaos? You'd be fucked, you decided, loudly. Unless you had some land, reserves, seeds, and a well. Then you could be self-sufficient and could build an Earthship to survive life off the grid.

My breath shortened again. Another nicotine craving was coming up quick and we were getting into deep conspiracy territory. I had been led to believe the intensity of the cravings disappeared after Day Three but this hunger that is not hunger felt as strong as ever and it was only a matter of time before you started getting loud about chemtrails or the inexistence of dinosaurs. I felt disoriented. Tired, weak, irritable. And my fingers and toes were cold and warm, distant and ample, clammy. A single cigarette wouldn't matter. It would relieve my discomfort and I could wait to quit until I felt stronger. Tomorrow would be better because—because.

I contradicted myself with a deep breath and reminded myself of my desire to quit. Of my target dates and my quitting strategies and how I thought the Warriors' understanding of mindfulness could help me. But then these were just plans, I said to myself, a rational structuring of an irrational world. Fuck. Think! Is it true that Thoreau's mother and sister did his laundry while he roughed it at Walden? You were confused, then understood. You admitted it. A community would be necessary. Did I want to chip in?

What I wanted was to kick everyone out of the store and go to the *Späti* around the corner and buy a pack of cigarettes and smoke until I felt nauseous. I knew this was foolish, so I excused myself and told you to keep an eye on the store. I ran across the street to the wine shop, where Norma was standing outside in her down vest and enjoying a cigarette with a four o'clock glass of Beaujolais nouveau. I entered the shop and left two euros on the counter for fresh bottles of still water, the third and fourth liter already. I had been drinking liter upon liter to help flush my system and aid a bowel movement, which hadn't been successful for days. All the water did was make my gut blimp. As I jogged across the street and concentrated on my breath, my heart was racing my brain on the Autobahn of Anxiety.

This was worse than a conspiracy theory. What did it mean that you had turned to me, your book dealer, to build a compound in the wilderness? I had a headache and through the headache a blurry memory of a mutual acquaintance saying you had isolated yourself.

Back in the shop, I sat down on the tall swivel chair and looked in the till for an ibuprofen. There was nothing. As my pounding heart and brain shifted into sixth gear, I remembered that our mutual acquaintance had made a point to say you were reading an Italian esotericist, whose blend of traditionalism and mystical thinking had been a huge influence on Futurism and Mussolini. At the time, this seemed unlikely. Your alliance had always been with the French avant-garde. Plus, your purchases had always been left leaning. Off the top of my head, which was aching, I would have guessed that most of the books you bought were published by Verso and Semiotext(e), two radical publishing houses. It didn't make any sense. Just one more cigarette. If I told you I didn't want to live with you would your isolation only become more, what's the word, definite? Would it strengthen your convictions? Damn it. Everything was jumbled. I could barely string together a sentence. And then there was that thing I wanted to say about the Warriors, what was it?

I tried to get a grip on myself. Listen to this, I said, as I walked to the poetry shelf and searched for a book to introduce to the discussion. I grabbed a small book I had recently read by Cold Mountain, the Tang Dynasty hermit monk, then flipped to the poem whose number was the same as my birth year, but this didn't help. I flipped ahead two poems to the year my sister was born, as there was no page 182. I took a deep breath and read the poem, number 84:

> To wander free among the mountains
> you don't need to buy them.
> For a steep climb you need a stout staff,
> and a good strong vine helps when it gets steeper.
> The pines beside the creeks are always green,
> but the rocks in their beds come in all colors.
> You might get cut off from all your friends,
> but in the spring the birds will sing for you.
>
> —translated by Red Pine

Holy shit! I could almost smell the pinesap through the dust of the bookshop and the hint of stale sweat. You looked at the "kitschy" cover of *Cold Mountain Poems* and laughed at my gullibility. There are no mountains, only private property. I wouldn't even be able to settle for flooded meadows or unfarmable moors after the cataclysm because these zones would also be owned. Whoever holds the deeds when order crumbles will protect their property at any cost. I didn't understand how the deeds would still have any value if there were no states but I was starting to feel like I didn't understand anything. You shrugged your shoulders then looked at the press' subscription card that fell out of one of the pages.

I drank some water. The water hit my abdomen. My abdomen tightened. I felt like I needed to fart, knew I couldn't. The fecal matter seemed to be lost in a secret chamber inside me and now the pain was more of a stabbing. I wasn't sure I would survive this.

You said that wasn't what mattered. What mattered was who claimed them. I wanted to protest but another customer wanted to make a purchase and I had to type the information into the spreadsheet: Dahl, *James and the Giant Peach*, 4.50; Le Guin, *The Dispossessed*, 7, new; Moyn, *The Last Utopia*, 12; and Liu, *Death's End*, 10, new. Breathe. I made my usual stupid joke about the children's book being for the adult and asked the child if the other books were for her. Like always, everyone was a little embarrassed and my canned laughter was flatter than usual.

The mother paid and you said goodbye to the family. I hoped you were the one leaving but I knew better. In the past you would hang around for hours and would ignore my pretexts to end our conversation when I would begin pricing up books and shelving them. My guess had always been that you were lonely. I guessed that you felt homeless in a way that I could relate to. Not at home at the nation you were born in, but not entirely welcomed in the nation you had chosen. And I guess this was why this whole thing was getting to me. I felt like I understood you as much as I couldn't and didn't want to. I knew what it was like to be overrun by my psychoses—or neuroses or whatever you wanted to call them. And I knew there was a way out of it, one that I had failed to execute so far, but which I knew was right and possible. The Warriors.

But then I blanked.

Where were we?

Right. Excuse me.

Survival stories are as old as Adam and Eve, and as a bookseller I've seen the fear of collapse be printed and hyped, year after year after year. When the world refuses to die in the ways these authors predicted, their books collect dust in the Used Politics section—I was losing the thread—I felt slightly outside myself—I found it again. There's nothing wrong with dreams of self-sufficiency but even hermit Zen monks who practiced autonomy always had to return to the city to make a living, at least intermittently.

Is that your *Rechtfertigung* for the status quo? you asked. That isn't what I'm saying, I said, but I wasn't really sure whether that wasn't what I was saying. I backpedaled. I understand the desire to damn it all, I said, but isn't it weird that every age says we are getting further from Nature and more dependent on the technological "fictions" populating our heads and that we express this through the same medium we condemn? You didn't see the connection. I tried again. Every email is a melting glacier—that felt good, poetic, to be remembered—so what should we do? Communicate through smoke signals?

Prepare for the bleakest of futures, you said.

There was a pause. A customer wanted a book from the highest shelf in the Used Fiction section and was scared to use the moveable ladders that can be slid from one end of the room to the other. I pushed the ladder toward the entrance, climbed it, and felt unsettled. All these novels suddenly reeked of annihilation. Was there a single one between Brönte and Capote that ended well? I wondered, is that what makes literature literature and not self-help? Halfway back down, my eyes dragged over Cervantes' *Don Quixote*, which pokes fun at the madman who wanted to revive chivalry and bring justice to the world. Here was a man who completely submitted to his own fictions once literature evaporated his brain, a man who was only able to die when he finally renounced literature entirely. Lost in thought, I handed over the book the customer wanted. *Junky*.

When I came back down, you were looking at Flaubert's *Bouvard and Pecuchet*, which was on display in the New Fiction shelf across the counter. I quietly laughed. You would surely identify with one of these two scribes who abandoned the world of literature and who tried to make up for their lack of practical knowledge with instruction manuals. But were you the optimist Bouvard or the pessimist Pecuchet? While you flipped through the pages, I pretended to answer some emails but actually looked at Reddit to distract myself and get a better understanding of the Warriors' loss to the Boston Celtics last night, which was totally uncharacteristic—we had only scored 88 points to the Celtics' 92, despite having all of Curry, Durant, Green, Thompson, Iguodala, and Livingston active. I scrolled through a couple of posts, happy to finally have a moment to myself.

It didn't take long for me to fill this moment with you. Everything was slowly coming together. You were the one who had wanted to start a reading group in the bookstore after your time at Occupy Wall Street, right? Or was I confusing you with someone else? No, it was you and you were different. You were a fiction, a legion of shifts. Thinner, you had ditched your Bolshevik goatee and had grown out your hair beyond a buzz cut. You had new wireframe glasses and your outfit was no longer limited to black high-performance gear, a black hoodie, and black designer sneakers. You were wearing an olive hooded Barbour jacket, a merlot Oxford shirt, and forest green khakis, and I felt like you looked like me, excepting the sandbags under your eyes. You looked tired. Actually, you always did.

Then I remembered the last time I saw you, about nine months earlier, in late February 2017. That day, the sun was shining, and Berliners were leaving the never-ending grey cave of February. You were very quiet for you and you brought in a load of books to sell. The shop was busy, so I got straight down to business. Our sticker wasn't on any of the books; there were none of our pencil marks on the first page and I couldn't see any of them in our order sheet. You admitted you hadn't bought any of these books about enhancing capitalism to accelerate its demise from us. I warned you we could only buy them at a discounted rate. You yawned, and agreed. I then paid you more than I was supposed to—these doomsday books were still hot titles at the time—but less than they were worth. I apologized. You shrugged your shoulders and seemed fine with the sum I offered. You took the cash and said you had to run.

That was strange. As was the simultaneity of the announcement for the lecture you planned to give on the Italian esotericist popping up on Facebook. I was too busy to really process this announcement but when I looked at the event page a couple of hours later, I saw that my poet friends were arguing with you in the discussion section. After getting the gist of the argument— that this theorist you planned to lecture on should not be celebrated as an "important figure"—I broke my code of ethics and looked through your order history in the spreadsheet.

Had we provided you with the Italian proto-fascist thinking? We hadn't. There was nothing that didn't match up with what I knew of you. It seemed to me that you might be reading this esotericist in the light of what was then current events, like Steve Bannon's rise to power and the President of the United States' inauguration in January 2017, and through the ideological bent I guessed you belonged to. The only thing that surprised me on that day in February was that your most recent order was two years ago. When was the last time you actually purchased something and didn't just sneer at books on the Chesterton sofa in the middle room? I forgot all about it but now in November something clicked.

You were not Bouvard or Pecuchet. You were a character from Roberto Bolaño's *Nazi Literature in the Americas*. You needed the money for your compound in the forest and were flirting with radical rhetoric as an outlet for frustrated ambitions or a form of imaginary revenge and you wanted to leave and/or destroy society as you knew it. You had turned to the far right out of resentment for your peers who never accepted your brilliance. A convert, a caricature, a villain, that I was, admittedly, embellishing in chiaroscuro for clarity. This didn't make you any less real—or dangerous. Dangerous? That seemed like a stretch. If I looked closer, you were the same acerbic person, only perhaps sadder and more evasive. You seemed lonely but not any lonelier than most of the other young foreign writers I know. Like them—or should I say us— you had often described feeling aimless and lacking community and I understood that you must have been aware of the weight of absolute freedom in a city where you could live on next to nothing and thus had no excuse to not do the things you came here to do. I was familiar with this and I found myself in my darkest moments almost agreeing with the you I imagined. The one that just wanted to be seen for the person you were or were becoming. Becoming? Now was the time to mention the Warriors. But somehow I couldn't bring myself to do it. It wasn't like I was enacting their form of mindfulness, so how dare I force it on you. On top of this, there were the guns. Were there guns?

Fuck it.

I savagely grabbed my bag, opened a plastic tin, and slipped something into my mouth. I started salivating and drank some more water. Tomorrow. I didn't care. I changed my socks right then and there. I felt good again. My neck was more pliable, my headache was subsiding, and the customers were thinning out of the store.

You laughed. In the introduction to *Bouvard and Pecuchet*, you said, Flaubert's goal was to show that "education, no matter what it is, does not signify much, and that nature does everything, or almost nothing." How stupid, *oder*? You have to admit it, you said, what with your lecture about emails and glaciers. I think I understand what he means, I said, all of a sudden feeling very awake and clear. It's like what you said about jet engines.

Just then, one of my favorite customers interjected. Had we ever read Marlen Haushofer's *The Wall*, which I had put on the display table? You hadn't.

I started hiccupping as this Lithuanian pianist in her 60s explained how, in the book, a sole survivor learns to live in an Alpine hunting lodge after an apocalypse kills, she paused, almost everyone. Living within a transparent wall that shuts her off from the rest of the world, she holds on to her previous, educated self because she fears she isn't human without it. I listened and drank some more water to calm my nervous system that was being overwhelmed by the nicotine in the Swedish snus under my lip. I burped. No one noticed.

As time goes on, the pianist said, the narrator eventually gets over her immense loneliness, inexperience, and boredom and learns to care for a cat, a dog, and a cow. In the end, she identifies more with the flowers in the meadows than with her previous self. There was a distant sound of birds. It was too late or too early for them to be outdoors. I won't tell you how it ends, the pianist said while fishing around in her handbag, but there is this: the narrator wishes we would have recognized that our only hope for a better life was love.

When did the book come out, you asked.

In the '60s.

She picked up her phone, blurted some forceful words in Lithuanian, and said, I have to go.

Now we were totally alone in the bookstore and I began to sing, "Love, love, love . . . "

What a load of rubbish!

That was a casual British colloquialism you had mastered.

Had I forgotten about the Grateful Dead hiring the Hells Angels for that concert in Altamont in '69? Had I forgotten that the Hells Angels had killed someone? The Dead's complicity with thugs was ludicrous!

Explain London then, I said, with a note of aggression. You looked confused. Hesitant, uncertain—then furious.

This is all such bullshit, you said.

Don't you get it? No one's going to save you but yourself!

We were still alone, and I grabbed the money from the till and the plastic tin from my bag. I excused myself and went to the bathroom. After I locked the door and sat on the unclean toilet seat, I realized I shouldn't have mentioned London.

Days before your planned reading at that other bookstore in Berlin, you were in London, protesting a protest to a series of events hosting alt-right thinkers. I only learned about your solitary counter-protest when I watched the videos that were posted in the bookstore's event page. In these videos, you stood in front of Nimrod Passage in Dalston, holding up a sign, defending the alt-right thinkers' right to speak in a democracy. When the camera got closer, your mysterious brown eyes burned with anger and disgust and hatred as protestors pushed and shoved you. I felt like you were being abused despite your calm—something my friends wouldn't agree with. Nevertheless, there was rage in your eyes that day, the same rage you just showed me, and I didn't want to incite it any further, especially at work. I also didn't want to be forced to defend the actions of some of my poet friends who had been at the protest as well as others who had lobbied to have your event cancelled here in Berlin. At the time, I had been worried that they were being swept up in repugnant groupthink behavior that had all the non-ideological characteristics of the fascism it was criticizing, as well as abandoning all nuance in the name of defamation. Secretly I doubted you were the Nazi everyone said you were. Perhaps you were only foolish, stubborn, naïve, or desperate for attention? Or perhaps I was only trying to explain away what I didn't want to believe—and so perhaps I was the one who was naïve?

Alone in the bathroom, I was mad at myself for pouring oil on the fire. It meant that I would be forced to hear your perspective and I didn't want to. I wanted to enjoy the Swedish snus under my upper lip, my failure. I exchanged the first for a new one from the plastic tin I had brought from my bag, the tin I had hidden from everyone and kept in case of emergency. Today seemed like an emergency to my addicted brain, the brain that bought a dozen tins of snus from the airport's duty-free store when I was last in Norway.

Much more than the last snus I had secretly inserted at the counter, I could taste the blend of cedar, orange, and juniper in the bathroom as I pressed the pouch between my tongue and the roof of my mouth. The nicotine walloped my nervous system. I took a shit. Finally. My head pounded with a renewed concentration that did not diminish even though I was aware that I was betraying myself and the goals I had set.

Damn it, I said. Then washed my hands.

Tomorrow.

I took off my glasses, splashed water on my face, then wiped myself with the dirty towel hanging next to the door. I smiled in the mirror. My face was crooked. The bulge from the snus under my lip turned my smile into a smirk.

Tomorrow.

I walked out of the bathroom and you were still there, alone. I yelled across the shop: I don't really want to get into what happened in London or that other bookstore here in Berlin. I know a lot of the people who were protesting you and I don't think they were right to force the bookstore to permanently close but your wording in the announcement was messed up and your responses kept stirring the coals. I got closer. I'd also be careful about placing the leftists on one side of the wall and you on the other if you don't want to make more enemies.

You then vented about leftist witch hunts, baseless character judgments, and the death of free speech. I said free speech is not very interesting. I'm interested in what the syllables mean. But you do you; it's your life to ruin. I walked behind the counter and looked at my phone as a gesture of disinterest and superiority. I saw that Melanie had sent a text message. We hadn't gotten the apartment we applied for. She asked how my day was going. I felt too guilty to reply.

When I looked up from my phone again, you looked dejected. Your forearms were flat on the high counter and your shoulders were hunched. Your head looked heavy. I almost felt sorry for you.

Hey, whatever happened to your reading group? You mumbled that now any kind of public event was impossible in this city. You had been vilified to the point where you might have to leave. Your eyes became darker, your complexion bleached. Any second now your lips would start to quiver. I asked myself whether my poetry friends would call me a fascist sympathizer if I decided to extend kindness to you. Could it be that you only needed an invitation out of the cold? That a steady stream of warmth would not make you so full of disdain? What was the right thing to do? I considered taking out the snus. I pressed it into my cheek.

Look, maybe you don't have to leave. Maybe there's another alternative, like the one the pianist suggested. You looked confused. And I seized the opportunity to finally bring in the Warriors' understanding of mindfulness as a way to counter all of your past resentments that you were still clinging to. Have you ever considered meditation, I said. You tried not to laugh but you did laugh. What, like mindfulness? Your scorn showed that we would have to backtrack even more before we could get to the Warriors.

* * *

Part of me silently yessed your critique of mindfulness from the beginning. This immediate distaste was not in relation to meditation itself. Indeed, since Melanie and I came together, I had taken to her practice and tried to meditate for ten minutes every morning. Rather, it was a kneejerk reaction to whatever is in vogue, a habit our generation arrogated in an attempt to remain distant, critical, ironic, and/or contemptuous to and with and from mainstream culture; a habit which is unaware, for all its self-proclaimed criticality, that this feigned neutrality and/or distaste is also learned behavior belonging to a particular milieu, and that could be magnified for critique and study for its entrenched beliefs, ad nauseam. In any case, I was hesitant to give mindfulness the time of day since it was a fad likely to fade from the cultural landscape of wellbeing as quickly as Slim Fast, Positive Thinking, or Tae Bo. After all, mindfulness coloring books were no different from their unmindful predecessors except in their marketing.

Added to that was Silicon Valley pioneering the practice as a way to get ahead in the cutthroat world of business. In June 2013, *Wired* magazine, which is more invested in Mountain View than Cold Mountain, published an article called, "In Silicon Valley, Meditation is No Fad. It Could Make Your Career." Noah Shachtman's article detailed how Chade-Meng Tan, an engineer at Google, had introduced mindfulness to the tech world with the course "Search Inside Yourself" at the Google campus. Tan's class, which sounds like treating your soul as an internet browser, was such a success that other employees at Google developed courses, too, with names like "Neural Self-Hacking" and "Managing Your Energy." The tech industry not only showed interest in mindfulness, they ingested it like a ketogenic-friendly shake of bacon, parsley, turmeric, and avocado. Why the idea that "the source code to spiritual awakening is open to everyone" might be revolting was best expressed by a caption under the main photo of the article, where a group of people is meditating on a rooftop in San Francisco. This caption proclaimed that mindfulness is "not just about inner peace—it's about getting ahead." In a world where emotional intelligence, resilience, and focus are all highly coveted skills that will ensure continued gainful employment, mindfulness promised to teach meditators these skills and to thereby make them more money.

To me, such a scheme turned self-discovery into a good business strategy; one that the managers could implement to illicit productivity. My reasoning was corroborated by Chade-Meng Tan when he expanded his course into a foundation, the Search Inside Yourself Foundation, for executives. At some point, Tan explained the purpose of the foundation to the *Guardian*: "If you, as the boss, are nice to employees, they are happy, they treat their customers well, the customers are happy to spend more money, so everybody wins."

Kindness is not negative but using mindfulness as a corporate strategy felt icky on three distinct levels. Firstly, and most readily, it sells enlightenment, making it a product that is hawked by the same companies that create emotional slot machines, addictive apps with predictable input and random payout. We are supposed to stay engaged with the product, no matter what it's selling, and mindfulness had been an untapped vein in the health industry. And therefore profitable. According to the marketing research firm IBISWorld, mindfulness' net gains amounted to more than a billion dollars in 2017. These are rather steep numbers considering pillows or chairs are optional—meditation only requires a straight spine and concentration.

Secondly, and this is leaning on the critique you delivered in the bookshop, if mindfulness were adopted in the workplace it would turn self-betterment into a micro-practice of efficiency and dedication—which the caption in the *Wired* article was suggesting, only in positive terms. In the same article, one Google employee described his mental state as being a defragged hard drive, i.e. functioning perfectly. In the process, however, self-realization becomes a tool of economic productivity. This is the old trick of Protestants dressed up in new language. Today, we learn ways of dealing with more stressful environments without changing the environments. By turning a blind eye to the systemic causes of injustice however, organizational life is depoliticized and individualized. Those who constantly have their drives frustrated by virtue of social and economic marginalization are regulated through such practices. And this, then, thirdly, which was your crowning achievement in the argument: mindfulness is a tool of oppression. Even if there's nothing directly authoritarian about it.

This was the gist of the sermon you delivered before you left the bookstore. Admittedly, I had some wobbly form of these prejudices when I first heard about the practice from a friend, a Google headhunter, not long after I returned from New York in 2013, and she had forwarded me the aforementioned *Wired* article. Since she was one of the most stressed-out people I have ever met, her depiction of mindfulness sounded like snake oil with a distinctly ayurvedic twist. But I still didn't understand what mindfulness meant.

Is mindfulness an intimately attentive frame of mind or a relaxed-alert frame of mind? Is it equanimity? A form of the Buddhist meditation called *vipassana* ("insight")? Or another kind of Buddhist meditation known as *anapanasmrti* ("awareness of breath")? Or is it a way to reduce stress? A way to just take it all in? A social movement? Or even, as a *Time* magazine article in 2014 called it, a revolution? If so, for whom? I'm borrowing here from Virginia Heffernan's wonderful article "The Muddied Meaning of 'Mindfulness'" in the April 14, 2015, edition of *The New York Times*, where Heffernan tries to clarify the roots of mindfulness and its affiliations with Buddhism.

Whether modern mindfulness is Buddhist or not is hard to parse, but it can be said with relative certainty that Jon Kabat-Zinn—who developed mindfulness as a secularized version of Buddhism as a way to reduce stress and cope with anxiety and illness at the Stress Reduction Clinic at the University of Massachusetts Medical School in 1979—has downplayed the connections between mindfulness and Buddhism from the beginning.

As the father of modern mindfulness, Kabat-Zinn states this quite clearly in the first sentence of his book *Wherever You Go, There You Are*: mindfulness is a "Buddhist practice that has profound relevance for our present-day lives" but such "relevance has nothing to do with Buddhism per se or with becoming Buddhist." According to Kabat-Zinn, mindfulness has instead "everything to do with waking up and living in harmony with oneself and with the world." The way to wake up and live in harmony is by "investigating inwardly our own nature as beings and, particularly, the nature of our minds through careful and systematic self-observation." He goes to great pains to suggest that such a practice is not necessarily "Eastern" or "mystical." He maintains that even Thoreau did the same thing when he left the city for Walden Pond. Nevertheless, Kabat-Zinn seems to have forgotten the substantial influence Indian and Chinese philosophy had on the famed author—or, if we want to be more generous, perhaps Kabat-Zinn was trying to sneak Eastern philosophy in through the backdoor.

According to Heffernan, Kabat-Zinn was uncomfortable aligning himself with Buddhism because "many of the secular people who could most benefit from meditation were being turned off by the whiffs of reincarnation and other religious exotica that clung to it." To appeal to them, Kabat-Zinn emphasized the scientifically proven benefits of mindfulness meditation.

Practicing mindfulness meditation is said to shrink the right amygdala, our fight-or-flight central station that controls fear and emotion. Scientific studies have suggested such shrinkage is a natural byproduct of meditation and it has been shown that mindfulness helps to develop a relaxation response to stress by quieting brain chatter. Such slowing down is achieved by focusing on the present and only the present, non-judgmentally. "This kind of attention," Kabat-Zinn continues, "nurtures greater awareness, clarity and acceptance of present-moment reality." That is, in practicing mindfulness we become more aware of ourselves and the world. When you meditate, you begin to notice all the thoughts and perceptions you have that are clouding the present moment. Which all sounds fine but by now you are surely wondering: what does this have to do with the Golden State Warriors?

Being in the present—mindfulness, or *sati* in Buddhist philosophy—is the El Dorado of sports known as "the zone." Positive psychology has identified the zone as a mental state in which a person is fully immersed in a feeling of energized focus, full involvement and enjoyment in the process of performing an activity. The zone is the complete absorption in what one is doing.

The practice of meditation was first pioneered in the world of basketball by Phil Jackson, basketball's "Zen Master," when he was the coach of Michael Jordan's Chicago Bulls in the 1990s. Having learned about Eastern philosophy from his brother in the 1970s, Jackson wanted to introduce meditation to the players on the Bulls despite Eastern practices potentially seeming esoteric. So, he tried to find a teacher who could connect with them. Jon Kabat-Zinn suggested that Jackson get in touch with George Mumford. Mumford, who was teaching meditation to prisoners at the time, had previously played basketball and had also been college roommates with the legendary player Julius "Dr. J" Erving.

Mumford, decidedly more comfortable with the Buddhist tradition than Kabat-Zinn, became the Chicago Bulls' teacher in 1993, right after the Bulls finished their first three-peat of championships and Michael Jordan went on hiatus following his father's murder that summer. As Mumford remembers it, the team was in shambles. "In the midst of this adversity," Mumford writes in *The Mindful Athlete*, "with team members in various states of emotional distress, Phil had to rebuild a team and bring harmony to discord. That's when he reached out and brought me to his training camp to teach mindfulness and help heal the team." One of the new members of the team that season was Steve Kerr.

Coining the term "mumfied" to describe how Mumford's teachings could affect a player, Kerr took to the practice, although he has repeatedly stated that he doesn't meditate on a regular basis. Instead, Kerr was much more influenced by an early mindfulness book that Phil Jackson gave him. *The Inner Game of Tennis* by Timothy Gallwey is so important to Kerr that he has reportedly read Gallwey's book every offseason for more than twenty years and also keeps ten copies on hand for anyone who might need to hear Gallwey's gospel.

In his manual for athletes facing the challenges of keeping the body and mind in tune, Gallwey begins with a situation that any Sunday touch football player or badminton enthusiast will immediately recognize. Think about the last time you played a game poorly and cursed at yourself for not performing well. Probably you told your body to do one thing and it did another and you were angry or embarrassed or disappointed. Gallwey's answer to this problem is to quiet the self (Self 1) who is giving the orders and to learn to trust the self (Self 2) who performs. For, "Self 2—that is, the physical body, including the brain, memory bank (conscious and unconscious) and the nervous system— is a tremendously sophisticated and competent collection of potentialities" that needs to be respected. If Self 1, the self-proclaimed dictatorial boss sitting at command central, is allowed to mope or become belligerent, it inhibits the performance of

Self 2, the supposedly lowly employee. As a consequence, Self 1's condemnations become self-fulfilling prophecies. In a way, Gallwey wants us to abandon the Oracle of Delphi's prescriptions of "Know Thyself" and subscribe to the Emersonian variant of "trust thyself: every heart vibrates to that iron string."

While this sounds simple, and it is, Gallwey admits it isn't easy to put into practice. The mind is powerful and capable of continually undermining the trust invested in the body. We have been trained from an early age to berate ourselves. Yet, Gallwey maintains, this is only a habit and "habits are statements about the past and the past is gone." In other words, if we would like to be our best selves, we must learn strategies to be in the present.

The Warriors under Kerr's leadership have developed one such strategy to stay in the present, called the "delete button." Put simply: you just start over. You press delete and erase the whole document. You start again and forget everything that happened, you focus only on what you are doing. By forgetting every play that happened before, we can stay focused on the present and not give Self 1 the space to keep bickering or congratulating itself.

Just how hard it is to stay in the present is something that Curry demonstrated during the beginning of the 2016–17 season when he snapped his streak of 196 games with at least a single made three-point shot. Sportswriters took this as a serious cause for concern and wondered whether Curry was slipping—never mind that making a three-point shot in 196 games in a row is quite the feat. Curry didn't listen or worry. He showed that even if you slip out of the present, you can press delete and, in his words, "lock in." The next game, three days later, Curry broke the record for made threes in a single game with thirteen. How did he go from zero to hero so quickly? Curry: "I don't overreact to games like that whether I go 0 for 10 or 2 for 12 or whatever it is. My process is the same, but I had another level of focus the last two days trying to get my rhythm back and see the ball go in."

For shooters like Steph Curry, there are no misses—there's only the next one that hasn't gone in. All you need to do is "Lock in! Dubnation," as Curry tweets before games. This is also true of the other Splash Brother, Klay Thompson, who can get hot like few others before him, because, as Andre Iguodala described him, Thompson can get "so caught up in a game that he's entirely unable to remember what happened twenty seconds ago." Thompson demonstrated his ability to go nuclear and only focus on the present in a January 23, 2015, game against the Sacramento Kings, where he scored 37 points, shooting 13 of 13 from the field with nine three pointers, in the third quarter alone—an NBA record for the most points in a quarter. (For reference, the average of points per quarter for an entire NBA team is around 27.) Thompson's historic quarter began with one of his classic turnaround mid-range jumpers, where he whips his right leg around in the air and lands wide to increase his balance, which was followed by a transition three, displaying his textbook jumper with its jump stop, fluid dip, and relaxed snap of his wrist.

Recognizing that Klay was in the zone, his teammates kept looking for him on every trip up the court. This continued even after the Kings players also became aware of his hot hand and started double- or triple-teaming him. When Klay caught the ball on a pass from Curry late in the quarter and had no space to get up his shot but still scored on an off-balance three, Curry, full of braggadocio, took out his mouthpiece and looked at the Kings defender in disbelief. There was nothing that anyone could do to stop him. Thompson was "unconscious."

Thompson's calm determination is on display almost every night and can often be overpassed in the hijinks of his other teammates. Even in the "BANG! BANG! OH, WHAT A SHOT FROM CURRY" Game against the Oklahoma City Thunder on February 27, 2016, Thompson "quietly" scored thirty-two points and kept the Warriors in the game in the fourth before Curry made the winning basket from half-court in overtime. But Thompson, who at some point took up meditation to help him press the delete button during a shooting slump, remains humble: "I don't know if I would've been able to break these records I've got in the past without the system I play in or the team I'm with or the guys I play with."

Pressing the delete button or locking in obviously is not the invention of the Warriors and they are not the first team to recognize its importance on the court (nor do they always achieve it). The zone has a long history, and if we stick to basketball, this state was best described by Bill Russell, the Boston Celtics legend and Civil Rights activist, in *Second Wind: The Memoirs of an Opinionated Man*: "At that special level, all sorts of odd things happened . . . It was almost as if we were playing in slow motion. During those spells I could almost sense how the next play would develop and where the next shot would be taken. Even before the other team brought the ball in bounds, I could feel it so keenly that I'd want to shout to my teammates, 'It's coming there!'—except that I knew everything would change if I did. My premonitions would be consistently correct, and I always felt then that I not only knew all the Celtics by heart but also all the opposing players, and that they all knew me . . . It seems less odd to me now. It seems more like, yes, that's the way it is, that's the way it should be all the time. We can be focused. We can be conscious."

There is a radical political and spiritual proposition in this statement, and one that Gallwey latently subscribes to when he writes, "Awareness of what is, without judgment, is relaxing and is the best precondition for change." Gallwey's claim here should not be overstated—being aware of what is is only a precondition. It isn't enough on its own; you must also desire to change your situation. In an essay titled "Buddhism and the Coming Revolution," the poet Gary Snyder has suggested: "The mercy of the West has been social revolution; the mercy of the East has been individual insight into the basic self/void. We need both."

Perhaps surprisingly, this "both" was fundamental to basketball's inception. Its inventor, James Naismith, was a chaplain and doctor in theology, and the game of basketball's original purpose was social and spiritual education. When Naismith, a Canadian immigrant, combined a number of different games he had known from his childhood in his "basket ball" (note the void) to keep young men engaged at the Young Men's Christian Association in Springfield, Massachusetts during the winter of 1891–92, Naismith believed, as he writes in *Basketball: Its Origins and Development*, there is a "great amount of good we can do through our athletics." By playing this new game, the young men would not be getting into trouble or feel alienated in the burgeoning city. In the YMCA, they would also be exposed to Muscular Christianity, where health was not opposed to spirituality (i.e.

ditch the hair shirt and show off your God-given guns). Muscular Christianity, an ideology that people like Theodore Roosevelt subscribed to, promoted the demonstration of the Christian ideal of honor and the development of character through physical exertion—a notion that goes back to the Italian Renaissance, which had drawn on classical Greek and Roman sources that maintained a connection between physical and moral character. Further, Muscular Christianity promoted the idea that you could glorify higher powers through athleticism, something that the Ancient Greeks did as well—in the process, some of those Ancient sports legends even became demigods.

Naismith believed players could learn a number of attributes while playing the game, including alertness, cooperation, self-sacrifice, self-control, and sportsmanship (which Naismith defines as "the player's insistence on his own rights and his observance of the rights of others"—something that sounds more like a civil obligation). There was another trait Naismith believed players could learn, which sounds strikingly similar to Gallwey's take on mindfulness. Called "reflexive judgment," Naismith believed players could develop "the ability to have the body perform the correct movement without mental process." Players can be unconscious, like Klay Thompson—and in the process attain consciousness. Understood in this way, mindfulness has always been a part of the game.

You might then think basketball was designed to create hyperaware angels out of players. Naismith wasn't naïve, however. Learning these attributes on the court does not translate to a virtuous life without effort and guidance. Naismith writes, "Games have been called the laboratory of moral attributes; but they will not, of themselves, accomplish this purpose." If players are to be changed by the games they play, they need to dedicate themselves to these principles off the court as well.

The egoist might nevertheless think that tapping into the zone is beneficial for having an edge over the competition. The egoist will thus train to get to that level of freedom. This is compatible with Silicon Valley's reasoning for teaching mindfulness. Applying mindfulness in this way can definitely work to a degree, but if its lessons are not embodied or are in conflict with other values and desires, concentration will falter. There will be a conflict between Self 1 and Self 2. There will be the thought of reaching for success and as a thought it will be outside the zone.

Remember Russell's description of the zone and his description of feeling connected to every other player. In the zone, there is no room for the ego and if you're really locked in, these self-involved goals are arbitrary. What is important is playing the game the right way, which comes naturally in these states.

Bill Russell again: "On the five or ten occasions when the game ended at that special level, I literally did not care who had won. If we lost, I'd still be as free and high as a sky hawk." Winning, then, could also be understood as a mere byproduct of the real goal of being locked in. Something we all can achieve. Like Russell said, we can be focused, we can be conscious—while being unconscious. And if we were, we would make James Naismith proud.

* * *

It was almost comical to see you. Almost a year had passed, and everything was exactly the same, although I had been making

considerable effort to be more mindful in the Warriors' way, trying to lock in to the everyday and pressing the delete button
whenever I made a mistake. The bookstore was bustling when
you entered. You scratched the back of your head and smiled as
if no time had passed.

I remembered how you had left that day in November 2017.
My boss had called my cellphone since I had switched the shop's
phone on silent (I barely remembered this through the with-
drawals' agitation) and he was worried—and also a little pissed.
As I walked into the back of the shop and spoke with him on the
phone, I remember making guilty jokes. My boss and I continued
to talk while I straightened the Science Fiction shelves. You hung
around the front of the store, at the counter, doing what, I didn't
know. It is hard to see the counter from that part of the store due
to a load-bearing pillar, but I started feeling slightly suspicious
when my boss asked me if we'd had any thieves again.

You had left by the time I returned to the desk from the
Science Fiction section. Strangely, the till was pulled forward. All
the money was gone. I ran out of the store in a panic. You were
nowhere in sight. What should I do? Call the police? Or admit
to my boss that I hadn't been paying attention? I ran back into
the shop and accidentally brushed the counter with my leg as I
reached for the phone. I felt a weight in my pocket and sighed.
I had put all the cash in my pants when I went to the bathroom
earlier. I was ashamed to think you had robbed us. Then I drank
some more water.

Like that day last November, I had broken my promise to
myself to give up nicotine forever when you resurfaced in 2018.
The night before, actually, in a future-oriented emotional turmoil

about what is described in the last few sentences of the chapter "Competition" that was compounded by my worry for my mother's health and security in a church shelter in which she was now living in Lake Oroville, California. The flames were encroaching toward my mother from the devastating Camp Fire in Paradise, the most lethal wildfire in the state's history, and she said she was having trouble breathing. After I read every report that I could, I had bought a pack of cigarettes for the first time in nine months. I smoked a number in rapid succession, laughing with the awareness that this didn't make anything better. I threw them away and pressed the delete button.

Now you were here, and I wanted to know what you were doing in Berlin. I had heard all the rumors. You had been hunted out of the city by the Antifa. You were working more closely with the gallery owner in London and were living with you parents in New York City, who had been bankrolling your life as a "cultural proletariat" all along. You had also moved to some unidentified place in Asia for reasons I couldn't remember. There were other claims being made and they all seemed conceivable, even the most sinister, especially after I spent a number of days researching all of your new and old web traces, the chemtrails where you defended the fascist stances of some of the last century's poets and thinkers or retweeted alt-right conspiracies and memes.

Last November, I had been very preoccupied with our conversation because I felt like I could identify with you to some degree. We were both writers from America living in a foreign country who didn't fit into any neat category. I also couldn't help but wonder whether I too wouldn't have gone down some such rabbit hole had I never got a job that put me in relation to others or stumbled upon the Rilke poem. Could I have harbored dark thoughts about others had I never rediscovered the Warriors or started playing basketball again? What would have happened had I never discovered meditation? What if I never found love? And what if I only appreciated these lessons cognitively and never let them permeate my skin and allowed them to change my behavior? What if I didn't do the work? This is all speculative fiction, but it still kept me preoccupied time and again.

In any case, I hadn't wanted to believe that you had swung as far to the right as everyone else believed. A part of me still preferred to not believe all the rumors I had heard about you. I wanted to believe you had bought property in Brandenburg, where you learned to take care of a cat, a dog, and a cow. I maintained a glimmer of hope where you were exploring a new life and had found love. In this daydream, you still had a cellar stockpiled with food, but it was to do some good in an emergency as you believed in morals first then food.

At first, I had reason to think my vision had manifested. You came into the bookstore smiling, loud and friendly. You asked about my family and wondered whether they had been impacted by the fire that was raging in California. When I told you about my friends who had lost everything in Paradise, you expressed your sorrow. I mentioned that my mom was now living in a church shelter near Oroville and that she seemed OK for the moment. You asked about her back, which shocked me. Good memory, I said, it's incredible. Her back pains had disappeared completely. She attributed it to Jesus, whom she had been praying to for healing. You laughed. I believe her, I said. I believe in the power of belief. *Na ja,* you said and smiled. You were affable, kind, and genuinely interested in what I had been doing since we last saw each other. But when I asked you about where you were living the whole tenor of the conversation changed.

You were living in London and were only here for the weekend. I kept pressing. Some friends were holding a conference on occultism somewhere in Berlin and you had flown over for the occasion. When I asked you who these friends were, you refused to answer. I noticed something had changed. As you spoke about yourself, you mumbled more.

Hard as it was to follow your narration on your current life in London, I nevertheless ascertained that you considered yourself to be hunted and that you weren't the only one. There was a whole world being suppressed by the mainstream media and the leftists. At my bidding for more explanation, you changed the topic. Who had ordered Ted Kaczynski's *Technological Slavery*? Just some customer I said, looking behind me on the reserve shelf. You said you'd like to speak to this person. Kaczynski was a prophet.

I asked if you still planned to buy a shack in the countryside and you said you were happy with the financial possibilities in London. There was nothing more that you would say to this except London was alive in comparison to Berlin. There was something about your relationship to power that went unexpressed.

You asked me if I was reading anything I could recommend. It only occurred to me later that this was a missed opportunity. Perhaps I could have suggested something that propagated a different worldview from the one you undoubtedly engendered. Instead, I suggested a book I was immensely enjoying called *Stream System*. I thought you might feel some affinity to this writer's biography. Gerald Murnane had retreated from the city and was living in a small village in Victoria, Australia. You thought he sounded interesting and you liked the title but weren't impressed by my description of the book's contents. You pulled out a book from your knapsack and insisted that I order the book for myself and the store's customers. The back matter was long and confusing and the only words that I could hold onto were traditionalism, UFOs, human evil, and spirituality. You laughed when I asked whether you were warming up to mindfulness.

Had I forgotten everything?

I didn't join you. It no longer mattered to me whether Silicon Valley had botched the job like Flaubert's scribes and failed to shrink their collective amygdalas down to their rightful size, small enough to not be worried about fleeing to New Zealand. I hadn't either. The cigarettes last night were proof enough. But now I saw things differently. I realized, like Kerr said, that we're all in the developmental business and that real change doesn't just happen overnight. I may have failed by smoking last night, but I know I can lock in again. I just need to hit the delete button. The important thing is to focus on the task at hand, whether that be basketball or serving customers at a bookstore or being present with loved ones.

Funnily enough, technology can actually help. As Alex Hutchinson wrote in the June 15, 2016, edition of the *The New Yorker*, the Warriors have made use of advanced analytics, sportVU cameras, strobe goggles, brain-zapping tDCS (transcranial direct-current stimulation) headphones, and intelligent sleep masks since Joe Lacob became the owner, just months after that Warriors game against the Portland Trail Blazers on April 14, 2010. On the surface, the purpose of using these technological devices is to enhance the play of the team and to restructure team strategy but there's something else being effectuated. In that article, Hutchinson quotes the neurologist Heidi Schambra, who notes: "tDCS may not merely trigger the placebo effect, as all treatments do, but enhance it." By enhancing the placebo effect, the players can overcome their bodies and feelings and thoughts through the beliefs the technology induces. Remember what William James said: There are "cases where a fact cannot come at all unless a preliminary faith exists in its coming."

There are two ways to interpret this. Either the Warriors are snuggling up to the cost-benefit analysis of mindfulness or they see it as a tool to help players achieve consciousness through being unconscious. Doing the latter does not occlude performing well for specific goals.

I believe the team's use of technology is not that of technological slavery, however, and that Kerr's implementation of the word mindfulness is more focused on consciousness. After all, mindfulness for Kerr is about the team being aware not just in the games but also when the players are at home. They should be locked in, conscious at every opportunity.

And we can help one another to achieve this. If we believe together. And this was the point Paul Wong was making, a fan who was the original "We Believe" sign maker. He coined the slogan in a very Jamesian way to reinforce positive thinking in the team and the fans and himself (his marriage was in a rough spot). When "We Believe" spread like wildfire, and Wong started making not only dozens but hundreds of posters to hand out, the Warriors turned another abysmal season around and made the playoffs for the first time this century.

And it's important for us to believe in one another, to get it together in action. This is something Coach Kerr is particularly aware of, and, what is more, he is aware that he can help others to lock in. As Andre Iguodala writes in his memoir, Coach Kerr would say, "Find the flow, Andre" whenever Iguodala entered the game and Iguodala makes it sound like it actually helped. Another famous example of when Kerr demonstrated the collective aspect of being conscious, that in the zone "you know the other players," was on March 5, 2017, when he gave Curry a pep talk on the bench. Curry was going through a shooting slump and Kerr reminded him that it didn't matter, that he was making an impact on the game anyway, his plus/minus numbers were through the roof. Kerr encouraged Curry to stay locked in and when the Warriors came back from the intermission between halves, he scored fifteen points in the third quarter. Fully aware that his star player's shooting struggles were meddling with his self-perception, Kerr stepped in, told him to focus on the only thing that matters, his efforts, and helped Curry press the delete button.

I wanted to tell you about this and insist on the importance of staying present in order to not go down such dark rabbit holes that only lead to death and despair, but then there was another interruption to our conversation.

Someone was looking for *Do Androids Dream of Electric Sheep?* and I walked with the customer to the back of the store. When I came back, I discovered that you had left without saying a word.

I pulsated with regret.

There was so much more I wanted to ask and understand and change.

There was also a poem I had wanted to show you, many times already in the past year. I felt like this poem could have shown us a way out of the dilemma we had been facing when I read the Cold Mountain poem instead. The poem I should have read did a pretty good job of demonstrating what the Warriors meant by mindfulness and what I believe is worth striving toward: awareness.

Li Shangyin's "Not Poor: Indications:"

Thoroughbreds sighing
Wax tears on candles
Chestnut shells
Lychee husks
Stacks of money, heaps of rice
Mother-of-pearl hairpins: abandoned
The jargon of orioles and swallows
Eddies of fallen blossoms
Songs sung atop a tall building
Books read aloud
Sounds of grinding medicine; rolling tea

—translated by Chloe Garcia Roberts

As a bad scribe, I had often been tempted to add a line: "Eyes unclouded from lasers." After all, you were right. Glasses totally suck.

Beginning, Again

ON THE GOLDEN STATE WARRIORS AND
THE SECRET OF BASKETBALL
July 2010–July 2019

It was hot and windy and the helicopter was waiting. The group of Americans were running late for their appointment to the Oracle of Delphi and the Greek pilot was getting impatient. The national aviation union was going on strike in a couple of hours and the pilot didn't want to get stuck on the other side of the country when he was no longer allowed to fly. He implored his passengers to board the helicopter, but Kirk Lacob's father refused. He was too nervous, too absorbed in his conversation with the other side of the world. Joe Lacob was waiting to hear whether his life was going to change in the way he envisioned. It was getting down to the last minute. The pilot explained his situation, then supplicated again, this time with different tactics. The Oracle is going to close, the pilot said, it's time. I know that, Joe said, then returned to the phone.

Sweating on the helicopter pad, Kirk told his soon-to-be stepmother that it was just like last summer in New Zealand. He was annoyed by the delay, so he distracted himself with Twitter. Kirk scanned a couple of links and liked a couple of tweets bashing the Miami Heat. Like everyone else, he was still shocked by *The Decision*, the live TV special that aired the week before wherein LeBron James announced that he was taking "his talents to South Beach" to join the Heat and build a super team with Chris Bosh and Dwyane Wade. *The Decision* was bound to be monumental and not only for the Heat, who were now perennial championship contenders. *The Decision* would change the dynamics of power between organizations and players, which had always been hierarchical, even if there were some noteworthy exceptions.

That power could easily be abused was something Kirk had learned at a young age when a coach from an opposing team picked on him because of his glasses. The middle-aged man had singled him out, called him a dork. No longer a fourth grader, Kirk wondered what it would take for an adult in his forties to bully a child. He still didn't have an answer at the age of twenty-three, but he did take great satisfaction in having beaten the man's team, the best in the league, and of having made six consecutive baskets—all while wearing glasses.

It's over, it's done, his father said. We're going to the Oracle. Kirk and his father's fiancée celebrated this monumental change. συγνώμη, *Sig-no-mee*, his father said to the pilot. I'm sorry. His gods don't live in the same time zone as Apollo and he needed to wait to see whether his fortune would change. όλα καλά, don't worry. His father wasn't worried, Kirk knew that, even though he was a lot poorer after this phone call. Millions upon millions of dollars were now going to disappear from his account. But then, the loss of liquidity had to be held in relation to his beginnings. His father was nowhere near as poor as he had been as a child growing up in

New Bedford, Massachusetts, or when he sold peanuts at baseball games to put himself through college in Orange County.

Kirk couldn't believe it. The Basketball Gods had smiled on his family. They weren't just going to the Oracle; his father was going to become one of the principle owners of the Golden State Warriors, a team that plays in Oracle Arena. This had been a dream his father had harbored since 2003.

Inside the helicopter, Joe, a longtime season ticket holder of the famously terrible team, asked his son to join him.

Just out of Stanford, where he joked he "majored in basketball," Kirk knew that if he accepted the offer there would be calls of nepotism. In the eyes of the world, he would be just another rich kid who had everything given to him without having to work for it. But he also knew that this would fuel him, just like the opposing coach in fourth grade did.

Kirk accepted a job that would initially be titled Director of Basketball Operations, and he would bring a new vision to the Warriors. In his first season, 2010–11, Kirk would persuade the team to start using SportVU, a camera system hung from the rafters that follows the ball and every player on the court, collecting data at a rate of 25 times per second. They would be one of the first teams in the NBA to use this technology as a strategy, and three years later the rest of the league would follow.

The helicopter lifted off.

It was time to leave for the Oracle. The one awaiting them at home.

And ever since, I've been irrationally convinced that the Lacobs learned "The Secret" of basketball on the hallowed grounds of the Temple of Apollo.

* * *

Almost a year had passed since their visit to the sanctuary at Delphi and Joe Lacob was getting ready to do something dangerous. During his first regular season as one of the principal owners of the Golden State Warriors (with Peter Gruber, who always wants to stay out of the Warriors' limelight), Lacob had approached the organization cautiously. He pressed ctrl-alt-delete and entered safe mode to isolate issues within the Warriors' operating system. But now, at the end of the 2010–2011 season, it was time to take risks and replace the old hardware with new pieces. Lacob, now standing in for all the shareholders in this narrative, fired the majority of the front office, then hired the fresh and independent Bob Myers as an assistant general manager in April 2011.

The basketball world was confused. Myers had never held an executive position, had never even been considered for one, and there were a number of experienced candidates who were on the market. It was a risk to hire Myers, but Lacob loved making gambles. It was his business. As a venture capitalist, Lacob had helped to establish infrastructures for companies that would later become the biggest corporations in the world, such as Amazon and Google. He felt pretty confident in his ability to smell out a winner. He could tell that Myers embodied the occult wisdom of The Secret.

Hiring Myers was a risk but a dream come true, this time for Myers. As a Bay Area native, Myers had grown up idolizing the Warriors as a boy—like yours truly. Later, when he worked as a sports agent, Myers would even represent Warriors players like Antawn Jamison and he always kept tabs on his favorite team.

It would turn out that Myers' lack of "experience" on the team side didn't matter. Within a year of taking the job as an assistant, Myers was promoted to general manager, which he excelled at. He would be named the NBA Basketball Executive of the Year the same season the Warriors won their first championship in forty years.

Nobody could believe it.

It was a picture book story.

How did the Warriors ever get so lucky?

* * *

Joe Lacob could be rather brash when asked this question. He would say their success had nothing to do with luck. The Warriors were light years ahead of every other organization, period. This now infamous statement in the basketball world seemed reasonable if you bought into Lacob's sense of destiny, but it could also be read as pure hubris, of which Lacob was skilled at if you ever put him in front of a microphone. In calmer moods—that is, when he was edited in pen and paper interviews—Lacob might take a different angle and say the Warriors' success is very simple. He ran the organization according to an authenticated axiom that he knew from Silicon Valley: hire the best people at what they do and then keep them happy. Myers turned out to be very good at what he did and then Lacob had to keep him happy. Another person Lacob brought on board was the seasoned Jerry West, who Lacob hired on May 11, 2011, as an executive board member.

West was a legendary player and later a vital engineer in

designing the rosters for the Lakers when they won eight championships during his tenure. West's shadow on the league is so immense that his profile is literally the silhouette of the NBA logo. Now that West was working for the Warriors, Lacob had to keep him happy, too. Which is why the Warriors drafted Klay Thompson in June 2011 at West's incitement. "The Logo" really liked Klay Thompson.

And, three years later, West didn't want to see Thompson go. The Warriors were getting ready to trade the shooting guard to the Minnesota Timberwolves for Kevin Love, an All-Star, unlike Thompson at the time. It was a risky move, but sometimes you have to push all the chips in, and Lacob knew this. West was having none of it. He had a strong intuition, if not an augury. *Do not trade Klay Thompson for Kevin Love.* He could foresee that the future of the league was in the backcourt, and in the Warriors' backcourt in particular.

He's a good kid, Joe, and he plays defense.

But he can't create his own shot, Lacob protested.

For Chrissakes Joe, defense wins championships! That kid's a golden retriever out there, chasing the ball wherever it's thrown! "The Logo" was livid. *That kid can focus! He's almost, what's the word, monomaniacal.*

West threatened to quit if Lacob got rid of Thompson. Lacob's happy-hire axiom was getting close to collapsing, but he stuck to his principles. He cancelled the trade and West stormed out of the room.

Don't ever doubt Klay Thompson again or I'll leave, I mean it! As he slammed the door, the echo of The Secret reverberated in the office windows.

* * *

From r/nba:

You're fucking kidding me. If that old bat hadn't freaked out, the Warriors would have never won their first championship? How can they always be so lucky? 42 karma points.

A comment to this comment: *They were lucky that Curry's ankles were as strong as cooked spaghetti in 2012 so they could keep him on a cheap contract and they were lucky Klay Thompson learned to dribble the ball and became an All-Star. Still can't dunk though [link to "China Klay" getting stuck on the rim at an exhibition court in Chengdu]* . . . 19 karma points.

A comment to this comment: *Don't forget they were lucky that David Lee was injured, so that Draymond Green could get playing time and become Draymond. I mean, it's crazy. They found Draymond in the second round [link to Draymond naming all thirty-four players drafted before him]* . . . *Are you kidding me?* 37 karma points.

A comment to this comment: *Maybe West is clairvoyant. Thank God he left for the Clippers when Lacob finally pissed him off. Lacob. What an asshat. "Light years ahead."* 8 karma points.

A comment to this comment: *Those spoiled rich kids don't even deserve their first championship* . . . *it was a fluke.* -2 karma points.

* * *

The Lacobs see things differently. To Kirk, luck is a misnomer. It's a probability, which can thus be governed. His father takes a more Protestant approach: you aren't born lucky, you make yourself lucky; providence is earned through hard work. Joe Lacob is a Jamesian—William not LeBron. It is easy to imagine Lacob channeling William James and saying there are "cases where a fact cannot come at all unless a preliminary faith exists in its coming" in updated language. What is more, Joe Lacob believes success is inevitable if you work in a collaborative environment where inclusion, trust, togetherness, transparency, audacity, and grit are the fundamentals. Stick to your guns and you will become the Google of basketball—which is admittedly off-putting.

Even more irksome was that the team's winning started to feel inevitable. The Warriors were going to the Finals. Again. And again. And again. And again. After the fourth time, you kinda had to hate them as a casual sports fan, just like you had to hate Real Madrid, the New England Patriots, or the New York Yankees. This is because sports fans indulge in a form of speculative fiction where the world as it could be is better than the one that is. Playing this form of mental gymnastics gives them hope. Every fan indulges in these counterfactual histories, those Choose Your Own Adventure stories, where certain destinies, bad trades, and injuries, can be reversed so that order can be restored to the world.

Warriors fans are no strangers to this.

From r/warriors:

What if we had kept Mitch Richmond AND got Chris Webber? Hardaway, Mullin, Richmond, Sprewell and Webber? With gritty AF Šarūnas Marčiulionis as the sixth man (OK, he was injured that season but just imagine)? That team would have been unstoppable. 26 karma points.

A comment to this comment: *Bruh, that team would have looked a lot like "The Hamptons 5" [meme of the Warriors players*

Curry, Durant, Green, Iguodala and Thompson, have their faces pho-toshopped over a bunch of rich yachtsmen.] 7 karma points.

A comment to this comment: *And they probably would have played somewhat similar—Kerr's "death lineup/Hamptons 5" (I hate that name) comes from "Nellie Ball," Don Nelson's offensive strategy of running and gunning. Those guys would have been awesome together.* 3 karma points.

But things don't work out like that and there doesn't always need to be a conspiracy. We could ask ourselves a thousand questions and pose another 100,000 scenarios but The Secret can't help but laugh in the background.

And that brings us back to the beginning.

* * *

Again, Don Nelson coached his last game in Portland against the Trail Blazers on April 14, 2010. In his final season, Nelson had fought too hard to achieve the record as the head coach with the most wins in NBA history (overtaking Lenny Wilkens and finishing with 1,335 to Wilkens' 1,332) despite his players being injured. Furthermore, he had lopsided preferences for certain players. This can be seen even in his final post-game interview where Nelson praises Curry but makes almost no mention of Monta Ellis, who had also played an incredible game, scoring thirty-four points with zero turnovers while on the court for all forty-eight minutes. Both of these traits were demonstrative of the hierarchical culture the new Warriors organization wanted to decommission. So, Nelson was fired. (Finally!) Then his replacement was fired. The Warriors started searching for someone with "experience." But like the Pythia's message at the Oracle of Delphi, Lacob's vision could not be simply interpreted as wanting to hire a well-known coach. That wouldn't be risky enough.

In 2011, the Warriors hired a head coach who represented their alchemical mixture of established veterans and fresh independents in the same body. Mark Jackson had had a successful fourteen-year playing career, where he was named Rookie of the Year in 1988 and an All-Star for the New York Knicks in 1989— and no experience coaching.

Jackson would teach the Warriors the toughness he demonstrated as a player, as well as the importance of togetherness. Often spiking his message with a strong dose of biblical fire and brimstone, his players listened to their coach, who was also a minister. They attended his sermons at his congregation, and gathered in the corridors of Oracle Arena, putting their hands together over their heads and shouting "Just us!" As they ran out on the court, a garbled version of The Secret faintly echoed from within the walls of the corridors.

That is to say, it would take a preacher man to exorcise the demons from the troubled team that played in Oakland and to call forth its true potential. With Jackson's help, The Secret got louder over the three seasons he served as a head coach and it started rumbling in the corridors. The Secret would slowly roar. It would create feedback and become distorted and work against the walls themselves. Cracking the paint, "Just us" would reveal other versions of The Secret still hidden in Oakland. Like the one from 2007, when the "We Believe" Warriors exceeded all expectations and beat the Mavericks—the No. 1 seed and Don Nelson's old team—in the first round of the playoffs. And, deeper down, under further layers of whitewash, from the year the Warriors won their first-ever championship in Oakland in 1975. That 1975 team believed in "togetherness" so much that they had the word engraved on their championship rings. "Togetherness" is but one translation of The Secret. But then, what is this secret?

* * *

Like other oracular pronouncements, The Secret is shrouded in mystery. And most teams get blinded by envisioning what they want to envision when they hear it. They forget that certain riddles need to be solved with dedication—physically, mentally, and emotionally—and you can't just pay lip service to it: you can't pretend to believe, you actually have to. Esoteric as all this sounds, The Secret is actually quite simple. It merely states that "the secret to basketball is that it is *not* about basketball." It's about chemistry and relationships. It's about taking care of your teammates and knowing that individual success is less important than being willing to work, together, for a common goal. As obvious as that sounds, it remains a secret to professional basketball players in general.

According to Bill Simmons in *The Book of Basketball*, every team that has won multiple championships has mastered some translation of The Secret. Their dedication to The Secret is what kept them in a position to win—which, it shouldn't be forgotten, is the goal of the game and the teams and the players. That doesn't mean that there aren't countless other teams who have also embodied The Secret throughout history. There are plenty of teams who were victims of a bad bounce or an injury or some other such blow of fate that kept them from their stated goal. But, the sad fact of sports like basketball is that we can only ever talk about these teams in the conditional. Or, they simply get forgotten. Like older versions of The Secret, which is as mercurial as it is substantial. The Secret morphs over the ages. "Togetherness" becomes "Just us" and other elements are included. We are living in different times and they should be met with different strategies. You inherit The Secret, but you must remember that as our language changes, so, too, must our behavior. Like poetry, you have to make The Secret new. It is always becoming.

* * *

Although Mark Jackson taught the Warriors grit and togetherness as his version of The Secret, he remained rather exclusive. Lacking transparency and trust, Jackson didn't fully match up to Lacob's vision. This can even be seen in the way the Warriors played during his tenure. Although Jackson would turn the team with the fourth-worst defensive rating (2010–11) into the team with the fourth-best defensive rating (2013–14), his offensive schemes relied primarily on isolation plays and post-ups (things he had excelled at as a player). This individual-heavy style was out of synch with the specific talents of the players on the Warriors as well as with the horizontal model of power the organization had adopted. As Erik Malinowski writes in *Betaball*, "In an organization that sought to encourage dialogue and hold people accountable as much as lift them up, Jackson preferred his bubble of authority." So, he had to go, too.

Jackson was fired after the Warriors were eliminated in

the first round of the 2014 NBA Playoffs by the Los Angeles Clippers. Graciously, Lacob tried to minimize the critique of his now former coach. Lacob used the corporate-speak of the tech world to explain the Warriors' decision: "There's a different CEO that may be required to achieve success at different stages of an organization's success. When you're a startup company it's one thing, when you're a small-growth company it's one thing, and when you're a mature company that's trying to reach a billion in sales—or in this case win an NBA championship—perhaps that's a different person. And we just felt overall we needed a different person."

That person was someone who had never coached, but it was someone who had been initiated into two different iterations of The Secret during the 1990s and 2000s. Having seen that The Secret never stayed the same, that it always changed its day-to-day interpretation dependent on the person who received and then delivered it (we are shaped by our experiences), this new head coach would create a new translation to take the Warriors further. Steve Kerr would construct his four core values of joy, mindfulness, compassion, and competition as his own version of The Secret, which would become known as "Strength in Numbers." These values condensed in the slogan became the foundation for the team's culture, not because they sounded good on motivational posters but because they were things that were factually close and important to Kerr's person—they matched up with his experience. In doing so, the Warriors hit hyperdrive and entered greatness.

* * *

On r/nba:

Look, I didn't want to have to do this, but the Warriors are just lucky. There's Klay Thompson going nuclear in the 2016 Western Conference Finals when they were down 3-1(!), Kawhi Leonard getting injured the next year by Zaza, and Chris Paul the year after that. Every year they won, at least one of the superstars of their opponents was injured. Don't forget K Love AND Kyrie were injured the first year they won against Cleveland. Forty karma points.

A comment to this comment: *What proves their luck the most was the year they lost. LeBron handed them their asses. Him winning a championship in Cleveland definitely cements his legacy. Don't @ me.* Fifteen karma points.

A comment to this comment: *SMH. Then Draymond cried like a baby and begged Durant to come after losing to LeBron. [Snake emoticon]* Twenty-three karma points.

A comment to this comment: *Actually, it was Jerry West who convinced the snake to come.* No karma points.

A comment to this comment: *Nephew. KD came because of the salary cap spike. SMH.* One karma point.

A comment to this comment: *The Warriors are lucky AF.* Eleven karma points.

A comment to the first comment: *GTFOH. We only lost because Draymond was suspended for Game 5 when he hurt LeBron's feelings and then Bogut went down with the knee injury.* Minus eight karma points.

A comment to this comment: *If Bogues didn't get injured, we wouldn't have played Festus or that flophouse Anderson Varejão in Game 7. Sorry Anderson. Still love you bro.* Minus one karma point.

A comment to this comment: *Why does Kerr have to be so*

stubborn? You win basketball games by playing your best players and not with motivational slogans. Two karma points.

A comment to the first comment: *LeBron would have never won if he didn't create the Heatles in Miami. I don't get the double standard. They were the first super team! They just hate us because we're winning.* Minus three karma points.

A comment to this comment: *And now we have the infinity gauntlet! I can't wait until DeMarcus Cousins comes back from injury! We're going to be Championship [Link to Leandro Barbosa meme]!* Two karma points.

A comment to this comment: *NOTHING EASY, BABY!* [Link to Zaza Pachulia meme]. One karma point.

* * *

The obsessive emphasis on winning in fan and media discussions often misses the point of it all. Winning is not merely a neoliberal project, or not only one. By focusing on the monetary aspects and using the usual war metaphors, it says more about the person making the utterance—our language mirrors our minds—than it does about the players, who dedicate themselves with their minds and bodies and spirits to the game every day for a number of decades. Winning is about achieving your goal. It's about clarity awakening, a release. Former senator Bill Bradley, who was a star forward for a New York Knicks championship team that knew The Secret, once said: "If there is any broader social meaning to the championship, it is . . . that it gives a glimpse of a better world—a world unattainable. A team championship exposes the limits of self-reliance, selfishness, and irresponsibility." Or, as Bill Bradley's teammate Phil Jackson said, "Winning is about moving into the unknown and creating something new."

* * *

The debate about the Warriors and their winning would continue until the end of the 2019 NBA Finals, where they lost to the Toronto Raptors. But almost no one remembers how the debate in the Reddit feed started: a picture posted on Twitter of Steve Kerr and his old coach Gregg Popovich eating together in San Francisco shortly before the 2019 Finals started. But then, that isn't how it started either.

It started in 2014, when Kerr was on the market for a coaching job and was even being considered for the position in New York where his other old coach, Phil Jackson, was now the Knicks' team president. Kerr was leaning toward the job in New York, but the open Warriors position was tempting. Besides being able to work with Curry and Thompson—who he could identify with as they were jump shooters, like him—he could be closer to his son, who was studying at UC Berkeley. The interest in the Bay Area was mutual. Lacob had always wanted to hire Kerr. They were golfing buddies.

When Kerr presented a sixteen-page PowerPoint presentation (titled "Why I am Ready to Be a Head Coach") and detailed the other people he planned to hire as assistants, his job interview proved to Lacob and Myers that Kerr understood the importance of an integrated, inclusive operation that also placed trust in others, transparently. Importantly, he wasn't saying all this because he was trying to win the interview. Kerr: "I try to keep things consistent with who I am . . . it has to be incorporated into my own personality." And the same goes for his four core values.

A brief interlude as an exposition of one of the many examples of Kerr being joyful: on December 15, 2016, Kerr addressed Craig Sager's passing earlier that day. A part of the NBA family and a good friend of Kerr while they were both working as broadcasters for TNT, Sager deserved to be honored that evening with a moment of silence.

Kerr, however, felt differently. Before the game, he announced to the fans at Oakland's Oracle Arena that Sager wouldn't like to be remembered with silence. Known as much for his ostentatious suits as his cheer, Sager never let himself be discouraged during a two-year long battle with leukemia. He believed that "the way you think influences the way you feel and the way you feel determines how you act." And he continued to act ostentatiously. After listing a number of things Sager loved and telling anecdotes about the time Kerr spent with him as a broadcaster, the Warriors announced it would be more appropriate "given the way Craig lived his life and the joy he brought to so many people to have a moment of joy" instead of a moment of silence. Kerr then asked the entire Oracle Arena to join him in applauding "a great man and a life well lived."

Roaracle erupted.

When Kerr was announced as the new head coach of the Golden State Warriors before the 2014–15 season, he was aware that he was inheriting a team that had become very solid. In public, he applauded their previous work under Jackson, and the players saw this as a show of respect for what they had already accomplished. The "just us" climate that Jackson had established didn't vibe with Kerr's vision of the team, though. He never told the players to stop their chant (which they continue to do), but he wanted the team to be more inclusive than the sign Jackson had up in the locker room: "mUSt be jUSt about US."

Instead of seeking conflict with contradiction, Kerr set out with his message from the beginning.

Before training camp in his first season, Kerr played a motivational video at the Warriors' training facility. According to the *SF Gate*, this video was "preparing the players to take a step back from individual honors and consider the team as a whole." Never released, the video remained a ghost in the machine, a flaming sword or some other such weapon from mythology. Its title: "Strength in Numbers."

I won't lie. I felt like it was my lucky day when I finally watched the original "Strength in Numbers" video. For years I had been obsessed with finding it. Kerr often referred to the video in interviews, and journalists mused on its contents as the Warriors picked up steam during his first season as head coach. With the best record in the league before the All Star break in the 2014–15 season, it was obvious that big changes had been made since Jackson's departure and that "Strength in Numbers," which also became the team's new marketing slogan, had been integral to their success.

Greedily, I searched for "strength in numbers golden state warriors video" for years and panned through every Google hit. I would watch all of the Warriors' promotional videos that had "Strength in Numbers" in their titles and would even listen to keynotes their management delivered to Silicon Valley firms while I did the dishes.

I never struck gold.

Then, Google's rankings changed in March 2017. The first hit was suddenly a page detailing the motto's creation story. Published right after the Warriors won in 2015, the website was a miracle. I read all the familiar information on the page and there it was. The unreleased video. I couldn't believe my luck. And I couldn't believe I had never found the page before—literally every other Google hit had a timestamp from the last time I entered the page. There was a catch, though. The video required a password. More enigmatic than having this page delivered to me after years of searching was seeing the password directly above the Vimeo link. Unbelievably, the creator even requested for the video to remain a secret. I struck it rich and was asked to renounce it. I did. And I will. But not without pinching a fingerprint's worth of gold: the first sequence of game-time action is of Andre Iguodala, who hits a corner three and then runs to his teammates, hugging them, jumping with them, celebrating, together.

This scene from the original "Strength in Numbers" video would prove to be emblematic. Besides asking the team to follow his four core values, Kerr's first major adjustment toward steering the team to the "Strength in Numbers" ethos would be to ask Iguodala to embrace the team and become the first player off the bench—or, as Iguodala's memoir has it, *The Sixth Man*. Normally a move like this would be interpreted as a demotion. A former All-Star and gold medalist at the 2012 Olympics who was still in his prime, Iguodala was one of their best players. Kerr wanted

Iguodala to consider the impact his leadership abilities would have with the second string on the floor, however. There should be no surprise this request came from Kerr. A role player for his entire career, Kerr knew how to have a positive influence when coming off the bench. Kerr was not asking Iguodala to step down, he was petitioning him to step up in a new role. Fortuitously, Iguodala agreed. It was another one of those moments where The Secret was at work.

* * *

That's the thing, the Hall of Fame center Bill Walton suggested to Bill Simmons in *The Book of Basketball's* epilogue: The Secret is not a secret, it is a choice. In a world where personal feats and eye-popping statistics will guarantee fame and material success, players have to choose to ignore these ego-stroking compensations. They have to choose to dedicate themselves to the team even if it means they will receive less immediate personal gratification. That's why coaches are so important. Coaches, Walton told Simmons, can show you that what matters is choosing to act in concert. And, coaches can create environments where this will become more likely.

* * *

With his assistant Ron Adams picking up where Mark Jackson's defensive crew left off, the offense was Kerr's biggest remaining question. To be able to play according to the four core values and achieve their "Strength in Numbers," Kerr retooled the offense, borrowing strategies from the famous coaches he had worked with and for and against—including Lute Olsen, Phil Jackson, Gregg Popovich, Cotton Fitzsimmons, Jerry Sloan, Mike D'Antoni, Doc Rivers, and, yes, even Don Nelson. He established an offensive system that would integrate all the players and encourage them to embrace one another.

Put simply, Kerr's answer was passing. Passing, Kerr believes, empowers the players and disallows them from being passive spectators while the star players go to work in isolation. Passing keeps everyone happy because they get to be part of the action. Passing keeps everyone focused because they can't simply go on autopilot. Passing keeps players compassionate because, well, sharing is caring. Passing is also one of the few statistics the Warriors continually monitor using the SportVU system that Kirk Lacob petitioned to integrate into the organization. Tracking all of the ball and player movement, their stated aim is to complete 300 passes per game because it statistically ensures victory.

But a win isn't just a win—at least not to me. Reducing basketball to a mere loss or victory denies the whole aesthetic dimensions of the game, part of its mystery. Although the Warriors have had plenty of ugly wins and even uglier losses since Kerr has become the head coach, when they are playing according to the four core values, their "Strength in Numbers," they create rich, articulate, and beautiful experiences like every other mythical team in NBA history.

An illustration from the "BANG! BANG! OH, WHAT A SHOT FROM CURRY" Game against the Oklahoma City Thunder on February 27, 2016: Sean Livingston secures a rebound off a Thunder miss, then dribbles the ball toward the half-court line, where he quickly passes it to Klay Thompson, who immediately passes it to Draymond Green in the post. Meanwhile, Livingston hesitates then makes a hard cut to the basket. Draymond finds him under the basket. Livingston can sense that he's drawn two defenders with him, so he passes the ball to Mo Speights at the elbow, who is wide open and strokes in an easy jumper. It was a simple play, but the quick thinking and interconnectedness were hypnotizing. Just like in one of my favorite plays during the Warriors' dynasty.

In a January 9, 2015, game against the Sacramento Kings, Curry makes the inbound pass to Livingston near the half-court line and then runs through the middle of the court. He gets a screen from Green, who steps back behind the three-point line. Green takes the pass from Livingston and rockets the ball to Curry who has cut past the basket and back. Curry takes a shot that doesn't go in but Bogut tips the ball, once, twice, thrice, four times and finally secures the rebound. Bogut quickly brings the ball back to the top of the key, tosses a pass to Thompson at the left wing. Thompson then passes to Curry and sets a screen for him. Curry barrels toward the basket then passes behind his back to Green at the top of the three-point line. Green passes to Thompson at the wing but Thompson is suddenly double-teamed. Thompson rockets the ball to Curry again, who has made his way to the corner. Curry catches, shoots, and hits the open three. As the Warriors' color commentator Jim Barnett said that night, "If you watched everything that just happened there, it'd have to put a natural smile on your face. The way they moved it. Beautifully done."

These eight passes and the movement from the players were beautiful. To really express the full glory of this play in writing would take five simultaneous narratives to chart each of the players movements as well as that of their defenders. It deserves a whole book. But this brief sketch at least intimates that the Warriors' players—who are working together with a remarkable sense of chemistry to find openings before they are even there, an act of divination—also understand The Secret that they have to work together. Which, even if they didn't learn it from Kerr they have him to thank for unlocking it.

* * *

From r/nba:

Whatever. SoKerrtes is not some great philosopher or Grand Master. He just has a lot of really good players on his team who know how to play basketball. Remember when "boy genius" gave his All-Stars the clipboard for that entire game in Phoenix? They don't need him. They'd even win if I coached! Eighty-eight karma points.

A comment to this comment: *Kerr wasn't even there when they won 24 games in a row at the beginning of the 2015–16 season. Luke Walton was at the helm and we've all seen how much he's lost as a head coach with his other teams. Those players don't need a coach. If they do, it's probably someone else. Don't forget, Mike Brown coached the Warriors for most of the 2017 playoffs when they were unstoppable. Kerr even gave the clipboard to Mike Brown to draw up a crucial ATO play vs Portland in OT in 2019. Kerr knows nothing.* Seventy-six karma points.

A comment to this comment: *Draymond also played way better when Kerr wasn't coaching. They totally hate each other.* Eighteen karma points.

A comment to the comment before: *Also the idea for "The Death Lineup" came from his video assistant, Nick U'Ren. Kerr's a hack.* 74 karma points.

A comment to the first comment: *The Warriors are just lucky. It's all because of /u/R_Dollaz's toaster! Damn you!* Fifty-seven karma points.

A comment to this comment: *NEEEEEPPPHHHHEEEWWW.* Forty karma points.

* * *

In a way, the Warriors haters are right. Kerr doesn't have to do all that much. He puts trust in everyone in the organization to do what they know how to do—and that includes the other coaches and players—and provides them with a system to enact it. Lacob had already hired all the best people at their jobs and now they needed to be kept happy. In my own experience, being happy at your job means feeling fulfilled in your work and being appreciated by your boss, something Kerr excels at showing. This doesn't mean that Kerr is only a jolly animator. He may look like the Southern Californian surfer boy that he is, but he is not some calm Bodhisattva. He'll even karate chop through a clipboard or F-bomb a ref for a bad call. Emerson: "Goodness must have some edge to it,—else it is none."

Kerr's greatness would be none if he and his staff were not excessively capable of making important coaching decisions. All the proof you could ever need is that their third quarter adjustments are legendary. In the last four years the Warriors played at Oracle Arena, they collectively pressed the delete button in the locker room during halftime if they had a bad first half—most teams, it must be noted, furiously strategized to beat the Warriors and they had to take their opponents' best punch for every game for years. When the Warriors would come back out on the court after halftime, they excelled, scoring around 30 points per game in the third quarter. Their highest point differential for a season in the third quarter comes in the 2016–17 season, where they scored an incredible 5.4 more points than their opponents over 82 games. The next year would also be astounding. The Warriors scored 5.1 more points in the third quarter on average and that season featured the highlight of them scoring thirty-two more points than the Philadelphia 76ers, on November 18, 2017 (tied for the fourth best in NBA history for any quarter). In this game, they overcame a 22-point halftime deficit.

Despite what his detractors say, Kerr truly believes that the Warriors are successful because of the four core values that embody his version of The Secret: "It's all foundational. It's all creating a culture and a foundation of strength and fiber. It's something that withstands the adversity that will hit, no matter what, and it will hit."

Kerr knows this from experience. He learned to deal with the hit at a young age: when Kerr was a freshman at the University of Arizona, his father was assassinated outside of his office on January 18, 1984, at the American University of Beirut. Back then, basketball provided some refuge for Kerr who was unable to attend the funeral since it was impossible to travel to Lebanon during the war. So, he took refuge in the game and played against Arizona State two days later. Then, in his senior year, Kerr also demonstrated his resiliency and withstood the heckling of the Arizona State· Sun Devils' fans who screamed "your father's history," and even chanted "P.L.O." (the Palestine Liberation Organization, which claimed the murder). With a desire to silence the crowd, he hit all of his six three-pointers in that game on February 25, 1988. He admits he played vindictively that night, something he doesn't believe in. He didn't have the system yet, but he proved that he was ready and willing to bounce back from adversity.

Later in his professional days, he would learn better strategies to face adversity and would experience the importance of culture when he played for Phil Jackson and Gregg Popovich. He would borrow a lot from both of them, especially the mystical notion of culture, which, again, Kerr believes is crucial to be able to move into the unknown, to be successful. As Jackson writes in 11 Rings, success is achieved in a franchise by creating "a culture that empowers the players and gives them a strong foundation to build upon."

This can only happen when "a synergy forms between the owner, whoever his president is, whoever the GM is, whoever the coach is. There's got to be a synergy where there's a trust. There [are] no walls. There is no territory. Everything is discussed. Everything is fair game. Criticism is welcome, and when you have that, then you have a hell of an organization. That free flow through all those people is what really makes it work. And that includes everything from draft to Os and Xs. Nothing should be left to one area—only to the president, only to the GM, only to the coach—or the culture just doesn't form. At least that's what's worked for us."

These last words are not from Phil Jackson. And they are

not from Steve Kerr or Joe Lacob or Bob Myers (but Bob Myers does have them saved as a note on his phone). These words come from another connoisseur of The Secret, who is excellent at recognizing it in others: the San Antonio Spurs' head coach Gregg Popovich.

Another Popovich globule of wisdom, this time on players: "We are looking for character, but what the hell does that mean? We're looking for people . . . [who] have gotten over themselves and you can tell that pretty quickly. You can talk to someone for four or five minutes, and you can tell if it's about them, or if they understand they're just a piece of the puzzle. You've got to be able to laugh. You've got to be able to take a dig, give a dig—that sort of thing. And [you have to] feel comfortable in your own skin."

Michel de Montaigne: "Natural inclinations are by institution helped and strengthened, but they are neither changed nor exceed."

Aware of some modern translation of this, the Warriors knew that they needed to find players that would blossom in their horizontal structure, their "Strength in Numbers" ethos. Over time, Jerry West and Bob Myers would reconfigure the entire roster and make such incredible acquisitions in the draft, free agency and trade markets that they seemed to be guided by divination. Through these different channels, West and Myers would bring in exceptional players like Andrew Bogut and Harrison Barnes, as well as future cornerstones Klay Thompson, Andre Iguodala, and Draymond Green. Hitting jackpot after jackpot, it wasn't tea leaves or Ouija boards that made the team more complete. It was West and Myers' selection process guided by their principle: "Size, then character."

The order here is not arbitrary. Just as there should be a synergy between all members of the organization off the court, NBA teams today are increasingly devoted to "positionless" basketball, where athletes are expected to be versatile. Players should be capable of switching on defense (of guarding other players who don't play their position) as well as making plays and passes from a variety of spots on the floor. Centers are shooting threes and point guards are setting off-ball screens. It is a change akin to the rise of the gig economy. One day you might be building furniture, the next day writing copy, the next working in a kitchen. In a precarious world, you need a garage packed with tools even if the garage isn't yours and you have to borrow the keys from a friend.

With their exceptional skills, intelligence, and athleticism, today's NBA players are subverting the traditional roles of the five positions on the court and the Warriors are the crowning achievement of this shift. But to get the competitive edge in a game where the players slide out of their traditional roles, the Warriors have sought tall players because it minimizes mismatches on defense and creates them on offense. As tall as a center, with the ball-handling skills of a guard, and a sweet shooting touch like few before him, Kevin Durant—who played for the Warriors for three seasons that included two championships—doesn't like being asked about his position. He often answers: "I'm just a basketball player." (For the record: he's listed as a small forward.)

The Warriors' dedication to the principle "size, then character" is obvious when looking at their rosters. They were the second tallest team in the league in the 2015–2016 season and every player on their roster from the start of the 2017–18 season was listed as being taller than 6'6" with but a single exception; the only player to remain on the team since that fated game on April 14, 2010: Wardell Stephen Curry II.

At the very mortal height of 6'3", Curry was an unlikely player to ascend to interstellar spheres of basketball stardom. Before being drafted, Curry was said to lack athletic ability in a scouting report that is now as humorous as a Y2K apocalyptic vision. Constantly overlooked or slighted, this thin Baby-Faced Assassin just kept grinding and it is his faith in God and love from and for his family that has given him the foundations for an incredible character.

With his boy-next-door charm, Curry has proven to be a rather even-keeled person who can accept the challenges of superstardom (read for: people attacking your person and your family). The Skyfucker stays humble, which makes him relatable, which in turn only makes people want to get even closer. Instead of just brushing shoulders with the stars and enshrouding him in a bubble of famous friends who have also made it in the world, he prefers to say hello to children. As the TV chef Guy Fieri reports: "So the game's wrapping up, Steph's getting done with an interview, and [my son] Ryder's next to me and [rapper] E-40. And Steph sees Ryder from about thirty feet away, and he goes 'Ryder! What's up!' He walks over, gives a little high-five, gives the kid a hug," and seems to not pay much attention to the famous chaperones. It's so wholesome, it's almost corny.

* * *

From r/warriors:

Most people don't understand what makes this team so damn special beyond all the star power. We know suffering. We've been at the finals for the last 5 years and we know celebrations, but we definitely know humility and humiliation too. We received a lifetime's worth in 2016. We kept our head up and here we are 3 games away from a threepeat. I can't wait for Game 3. Eight karma points.

A comment to this comment: *We earned it regardless. Fuck all these haters and their increasing standards of "what's a real championship." Them bitches mad because they rooting for bad teams. Fuck the whole r/nba, fuck the media, fuck all the haters. KD is out, Klay is hurt, Looney is hurt too and they don't ever let us off the hook. But they let all those Raptors fans off the hook for dissing Curry's wife? Whatever. When we win, they'll still say it's luck but we believe in "Strength in Numbers." They said we couldn't do it when KD went down in the first round, we fucking did. They said Boogie wouldn't play again this season, he is. They said he'd be a liability, he isn't. They said we had no depth. Tell that to Cook last night. What these people fail to understand is we are on a motherfucking mission. LET'S GO DUBNATION. WE BELIEVE. 212* karma points.

A comment to the first comment: *GTFOH. They make millions of dollars to play a children's game. They don't have problems. You know what's a problem? Not being able to afford your child's medical bills. 438* karma points.

A comment to this comment: *[Deleted by user]* Minus 119 karma points.

A comment to this comment: *I have one MF. But Google won't give me a full contract with health insurance. I'm still 'under evaluation,' three years later. Like everyone else in my division.* Three silver medals, two gold, 1.1k karma points.

A comment to the first comment: *We lost. It's over.* 0 karma points.

* * *

Or, alternatively, it's only beginning. After some bumps on the road, the four core values of the Golden State Warriors are still unfolding. This isn't always linear. Sometimes you need to start over.

Compassion

More than two years had passed since I made the decision to live according to the Warriors' four core values and I was still very far from achieving my goal. But I had worked my way through joy and mindfulness in principle and had even enjoyed many moments when I knew that they were being experienced. There were certain flow states that took over when spending time with Melanie or at work at the bookstore or in the U-Bahn or doing the dishes where I was only doing whatever I was doing. And I also had noted that I was living more joyfully as I was more active and not just wallowing in the past. Still, I was rather clueless about the other two values and how they could be integrated in a practice together. It seemed to me that compassion and competition were very much in contention.

Seeing as competition was almost self-explanatory in the context of a sport like basketball, I had focused many months of thought on compassion and how it would have to be rendered to fit within the four lines of the court while also remaining valid outside of them. I did this first with my reasoning, looking into compassion's meaning, and assembled notes in countless documents. But I only discovered that I had already experienced some version of what the Warriors meant by compassion—for the quick answer, flip to page 183—after I got off the phone with Luciano on February 9, 2018. Luciano, a Sardinian native who moved to California in the late 1990s, is a composer and my only remaining close friend in California that I've kept in frequent contact with. On that Friday we talked about the time we separate times we spent in San Francisco in the late 1990s, he in the Castro scene and me in the Bay Area rave scene, and we were surprised we never met as these scenes often overlapped.

I just wrote "close friend in California" two sentences ago, but, in fact, Luciano was currently living in Maine. While we spoke via WhatsApp call, he was complaining about his glorified form of homelessness, the nomadic existence of moving from one artist colony to another. He missed the simple things I took for granted at the apartment I was trying to move out of, like knowing where the supermarket and post office were and not having to figure out how to do the laundry. On the phone, Luciano briefly regretted leaving Crockett, the last town he had lived in in California, where he had had a studio apartment with a piano. I asked him what had happened to the piano and he told me it had been rented and that his remaining possessions were in his friend Josh's garage in Piedmont.

I knew Josh mostly from Luciano's stories and from his occasional comparison of us, whom he called his two best friends. My closeness to Luciano made me feel close to the man I could only see in stubbled outlines in my mind's eye, but Luciano assured me that Josh and I were like an actor and his photo double. We didn't perfectly resemble one another but it was close enough for close-ups of hands or long-lens images of our backs. Or, as Luciano said on another occasion, we were fraternal, not identical. But we were definitely twins.

Unable to verify this similarity from such a great distance, I nevertheless knew a lot about Josh from my conversations with Luciano over the years, and I also knew something very important and private about him. I knew that Josh had lost his fiancée in the Ghost Ship fire on December 2, 2016, that tragic night where thirty-six people died when a fire broke out in a warehouse that was hosting an illegal rave in the East Bay. I also knew that this loss had been crushing.

Luciano mentioned on the phone in February that Josh might be drinking again. He wasn't responding to any of Luciano's text messages and he never picked up the phone. I asked Luciano when the last time had been that he spent time with Josh and he answered, *That Christmas, the one I told you about, the first one without Donna.*

Luciano and I continued our conversation about the Ghost Ship fire, which I had closely followed, but we moved on to talk about my old rave days and our plans to meet three months later at his next residency in Europe. I was excited to finally see him. We hadn't spent time together since we met at his residency in Venice in 2017.

But Josh stayed with me even after we hung up the phone. And his story—or my version of it—would bring me very far from what compassion means for the Warriors, I would get closer than ever before. What I mean is that after Luciano and I talked on the phone I was sleepless, distraught. That night, I had the following vision, which I typed up on Melanie's sofa, a vision that I realize is another funhouse mirror of myself. We are fraternal, not identical. But we are twins. The cantsleep.docx text:

The calendar, temperature, setting, intentions, all of it, irrelevant. In this scrambling of now and then that begins with stale sweat in the morning, it is always the same, an eternity of blanks and more blanks and numbness. With a future that is wretched and spent or hopeless, and out of a past that was lousy and tough but tender, mutual. These are the parameters of yesterday and today and tomorrow and it is unbearable. That it begins, the day, and there is no way to escape it, even as the night gets further away and the disbelief is fading. Ebbing into sadness. The sadness that was already there, that never changes. That has stayed the same. In this world and of it but also from beyond. From going beyond, from leaving, that comes back every day with the day, the day that cannot be denied or deferred or avoided. Not even through sleep. Sleep only brings the next day closer. The day that remains the same, unable to be outwitted or beaten.

Not that Josh can believe it. Lately, he has tried to beat the undefeated day by moving very quickly, first thing in the morning. To wake up and rub the sleep out of his eyes then leave the house without brushing his teeth has made him smile. He is not going to let the day drag him down, deeper into another trouncing. He is going to get ahead of it and sprint out of the gates toward the unknown that maybe awaits him. There is an optimistic precision to his rushed sequence of leaving that the clock's correlated variance fails to convey. The clock may read 6:14, 10:07, or 11:26, but it is always the same. He wakes up, rubs his eyes, and changes his shirt. He drinks a glass of water filled with magnesium powder then bounces out of the house. Then he sits for some stoic minutes in the driver's seat, waiting for his carburetor to stop clicking. When it does, he honks twice and cautiously backs out of the driveway. This is a habit his ex-wife never liked; she doesn't understand it. There should be no need to lubricate the truck's engine in the Bay Area's Mediterranean climate. They are not living in the deep tundra. Then, the day before yesterday, she divined why he sits in the driveway, glumly burning excess petrol. He doesn't want to go where he is headed. He never used to leave so slowly.

Day after day, she watches this sad scene through the cracked blinds. She waits for him to honk and evacuate her range of vision before letting herself into his side of the duplex. There is no need to use the key. In his excitement, he always forgets to lock up after himself. This annoys her more than she would like it to, but she justifies being upset by staring at the key to her apartment hanging next to the refrigerator, which is clearly visible upon entry. Up until now, she has stopped herself from removing her key or mentioning his carelessness. After all, she is the one breaking into his apartment and she doesn't want to sound like she is scolding him. If she did, she would have to deal with the consequences. Fragile, he might accuse her of being intrusive and lash out like he used to. It's a habit he never grew out of: feeling attacked and attacking as retribution. Going on the offensive as the best defensive strategy while distancing himself from his emotions. Not present but not going away either.

He could never handle what he called his space being invaded just as much as he could never actuate the thought of leaving, of floating alone in the space he said he needed. This is why she let him move in next door all those years ago, even though they broke up long before it. She knows this arrangement is something the neighbors whisper about, but he almost always pays his rent on time and she likes having him around. He is funny, good company, and, in a way, family. She likes it. Especially now. When he could use all the warmth that is given.

In any case, in his apartment, alone, she turns off the lights and radio and television, then goes against her better judgment, leaving his swelling mess of wrappers and bottles and unwashed dishes *ibidem*. She is trying to mother him less from her side of the duplex despite this difficult period.

Knowing all this, she grapples with tolerance and sympathy and poise and almost feels guilty for turning off the clashing voices from the radio and television for her own benefit. Then she thinks of the price of it, for the environment, this wasted electricity, light and vibrations. Besides, he never seems to notice when the house is quiet when he returns home. He is yet to mention his established equilibrium of voices being disrupted.

She turns everything off and locks the door on her way out. Then she texts him from her side of their shared wall. She asks if he needs anything from the supermarket. She doesn't expect him to answer. She considers bringing him a rotisserie chicken. It was always his favorite.

When he returns from the crime scene, hours later, he is impatient and spaced out. He puts another bagged sandwich he couldn't finish down on the table then rotates the Venetian blinds' levers to suspend the day's progression. This is when he begins to render the rooms and memories into writings and pencil drawings, which he will later file when he rifles through a shambolic archive of printouts, clippings, and sketches that have been acquired and preserved and studied in the duplex's semi-darkness as he tries to establish the cause of his misery with the same irrefutability as the laws of thermodynamics— laws that he has dedicated himself to with increasing intensity. More than a physicist or librarian or architect, however, his grief has made him an author. But the scenarios he has penned lack the conclusiveness of an investigative paper or a blueprint for the future. They are more reminiscent of a Choose Your Own Adventure story, those destinies that can be carefully elected and reversed by flipping through a preferred combination of pages, events.

The imagined tangibility of constructing an uncharred future, of reversing the reconstructions of pathways and possible causes in the warehouse's labyrinth of alcoves and partitions, awards him the only warmth he is willing to accept that doesn't come from the spirits, the whiskey he administers with each twist of the blinds as he shuts out just enough of the afternoon light to simulate the morning.

Time is spent like this. Wanting to understand and change what happened and failing to, being unable to. All he can do is suspend the day to a time before, a time when everything was still possible. That and numb himself, recreate. Write the pages where she survives the fire or those that expose its origins. Regrettably, these latter pages have remained mostly blank, scratched out, or thrown away. The cause of the fire remains unknown to him, the authorities or survivors. He is unable to admit it, not even to himself, but early in the evening when the blinds are still drawn and he is already inebriated, this open case gives him faith. If there is nothing that started the fire, there is no fire. It is the next morning and she is still alive.

This conjecture never happens before his third glass of bourbon, which is usually when he checks his phone. There he sees that his ex-wife has asked him to join her and her partner for dinner. His reply an hour after her text suggests he isn't hungry but is grateful for the invitation. Maybe tomorrow. She replies immediately that he's welcome to come over for leftovers if he changes his mind. There's also something for him in his fridge if he gets hungry later. He is annoyed that she entered his side of the duplex without asking but thanks her. Then he opens the bag that is still full on the table. He wolfs down the cold pastrami sandwich from lunch, leaving the crumbled bag on the table. There is no time to eat properly, there is too much to unravel.

As the evening cools into darkness, he opens the blinds and turns on the lights and radio and television. To experience how the newsrooms filter the continuous stream of information into a dawning conclusion is what he wants from them but he is continuously disappointed. Two weeks prior, the newsrooms reported on almost nothing except the event. Now they know less about the fire than him. It is repulsive to hear how their nightly features have moved on to a world he is unable to consider, not now, never. As time progresses, it is as if everyone has forgotten what happened. They are all focused on other catastrophes, headlines, and places of conflict. On the world that is full of harms and needs and misdeeds. He takes this to mean there is nothing special about this recent tragedy except that it is his. Nevertheless, every other story leads him back to the pain he is living—a world of trauma cannot be comprehended when you're dealing with your own.

Sitting at his desktop computer again, he opens the internet. The browser's autofill leads him to the memorial page where the tragedy is remembered. He reads through some of the most recent entries and considers writing something encouraging for those mourners he doesn't know from the site, but he doesn't know what to say that hasn't been said already. It is difficult to not speak in platitudes. To not have a language that is flat, plastic, and cold when you feel flat, plastic, and cold. When you are alone.

He drinks some more whiskey, which warms his organs, then gauges the bottle's progress. Another pour at most. At least he doesn't have to leave tonight to buy another bottle and risk getting a DUI. There is one more bottle in the cupboard and another under the sink, a strategy of accumulation initiated on a previous day when he picked up his daily sandwich at the supermarket's deli.

This has been the biggest change in the past days of the week. The amount of alcohol required to enter the tomb of dreamless sleep, the numbing gift he is all too happy to receive, has multiplied as it has become less effective. Lately, after a bottle of whiskey, his face is bloated in the morning and his calves are tight. It's like he went on a long trek through the redwoods in Marin County and didn't stretch before or after. In contrast to much else, this is something old, familiar. He always had the habit of kicking in his sleep after having too much to drink. It is a metronomic gesture of denial or attempted escape that amounts to nothing. Only fog in the morning. Hangovers. That have grown worse by staying exactly the same. The day.

The day bathes his face through the open blinds and he rubs the sleep out of his eyes. He pours some magnesium powder into a glass of water for his sore muscles and hangover. He is in another day with bad breath and a sweat-soaked t-shirt. He gargles the orange-flavored glass of water, changes his shirt to the one he wore two days before. Or is it fresh, clean? Smelling it, then putting it on, he notices that his shoulders are sore from sleeping on the couch again. And again, he picks up his keys from the table, warms up his truck in the perpetual morning, and drives the five miles from Piedmont to stare into the hole.

Today is the same, even though it's Christmas. Which, if he were to think about it, would actually be a small miracle. If he were to pay any attention to the date, he would have marveled at the fact that the day stayed exactly the same on this one dedicated to festive merriment, the first without Donna. A week ago, the last time he looked at the calendar, the lack of gravity on Christmas would have been cause for celebration. He would have given almost anything to not feel totally destroyed during the holidays. This desire to be numb to Christmas had been preceded by the fear the week before, when he dreaded the possibility of the day ever coming into existence. Now that he has adjusted to living by another calendar, Christmas is just Day 23, as senseless as any other that preceded it.

Sitting in his truck, he is about to honk his horn when he sees Luciano get out of his car. Josh turns off his truck and greets him. He acts as if he didn't forget their plans to have lunch together and says he couldn't remember if they were supposed to meet at the restaurant. Luciano doesn't notice or mind and apologizes for not having a present. Josh smiles, doesn't care. He doesn't have a present either. Back when Christmas was special, this was a tradition, their getting together and not giving presents, only presence. It had always been enough to just spend the holidays together but then Donna was still there, and Luciano and Troy were still together.

Luciano hops in.

Without Donna there, they are here now, in a Vietnamese restaurant in East Oakland. The kind of place whose laminated images of numbered dishes has faded and warped into a single soupy reality, no longer distinguishable or comprehensible from time's unvanquished transition. They're talking about Donna's final services again, which they had attended in Chico with Troy. Josh is playing back the reverend's impressions of the flower arrangements, the blossoms in the darkness. He is going into great detail, transfixed on the purple thistles mixed with white roses at the entrance. This is another moment stuck on repeat, a scratch in the CD, that cannot be skipped without losing the whole tenor of the dirge he is forced to endure.

Luciano listens. He is still troubled by Donna's death and by what it has done to his dear, living friend. He tries to dampen the impact of reality with encouragement and speculation that Josh doesn't hear.

When their soups arrive, Josh reveals out of nowhere why her body was identified before all the others. It was her recent DUI, her fingerprints in the criminal justice system. This information escapes automatically, as if he were only a medium for the words that needed to be spoken.

Do you want to go see it?

Luciano is shocked.

The two of them have synchronized thoughts.

He agrees and they leave, their soups barely eaten.

Out in front of what remains of the Ghost Ship, Josh recreates the situation for the thousandth time, indicating the approximate location of makeshift rooms as well as pointing to the telephone pole that the warehouse's power was stolen from. He explains what he has learned about electricity and fires and how the people were trapped in the smoke on the second floor. Other mourners who Josh knows listen. They inform him of the latest developments before the police stopped investigating for Christmas. They had heard from someone who had knowledge of the investigation that the fire started in the sound system. This would mean the music killed them, a possibility Josh had failed to consider in all the different schemes he had worked through in the evenings. He had been sure that the faulty sockets, frayed cords, or antique lamps were the most likely culprits. As Josh takes in this new information, someone relays an opinion from another source: none of this would have happened had the sound technician not been so negligent. If he had had better control of the board, everyone would still be living.

Luciano blushes. He finds this hard to believe. The technician, Barrett, was a friend and Luciano had entrusted Barrett with the soundboard for his own concerts on a number of occasions. Barrett had always been very attentive to Luciano's needs as a performer as well as to the space they were in, its limitations. The other mourners backpedal. They apologize. They know Barrett had also lost his life. Maybe he wasn't fully aware of the danger. Maybe that asshole, the space's main tenant, didn't inform him of the warehouse's limitations. One mourner says they'll just have to wait for the official reports before anything is certain.

This is what Josh is afraid of. It makes him restless, desperate and furious. What Josh needs is a sense of certainty. Not the countless situations his grey space has painted as to why Donna couldn't escape the smoke-filled corridors, the corridors that became her lungs.

Grief searches for firmness in the haze of whys and what ifs yet every piece of evidence has melted into more questions, more riddles, a darkness that cannot be interpreted. Why couldn't the fire station, a block away, stop the blaze in time to save their lives? And why weren't there more fire extinguishers in a space that had been haunted by smaller fires in the past? Most importantly: why had the party been here at all? Other mourners had said the Ghost Ship was the third choice for a venue and Josh was absolutely certain that the label, 100% Silk, would have approached him first if he still had his space. If only he still had his space. This would have never happened. Of that he was certain. His fiancée would still be here. If only. What if.

End of cantsleep.docx.

* * *

But I was still awake, thinking about the fire, which, as an ex-raver from the Bay Area scene and a devoted follower of the label 100% Silk (whose artists had thrown the party at the Ghost Ship), deeply disturbed me. Why? Not because I thought I would have been at the fire and could have died, even though I attended many 100% Silk nights here in Berlin, but because of the inability to find a place called home. I opened another document and multiple saved tabs, and started writing.

Stillcantsleep.docx:

On December 2, 2016, 36 people lost their lives in the Ghost Ship warehouse fire in Fruitvale, California. Those who died at an electronic music party were teachers, musicians, poets, students, publishers, jewelry designers, healers, artists, technicians, baristas, and music lovers. Daughters and neighbors, sons and lovers, these community members were eulogized by their fellows and family members in the Bay Area and beyond, as well by the international media, which took more interest in this story than in previous conflagrations in clubs like The Station, Club Colectiv, Wuwang Club, or Kiss where one hundred, twenty-seven, forty-three, and 238 people died in the years 2003, 2015, 2008, and 2013. While there are many potential reasons for this, some more charitable to the newsrooms than others—like the fact that the tragedy in Oakland was not caused by pyrotechnics, a flirting with danger that occurred in West Warwick, Bucharest, Shenzen, and Santa Maria—the follow-up articles streaming in for weeks suggested that the Ghost Ship fire illuminated a murky aspect of contemporary living: namely, the relationship between housing and city development. That is, the vulnerability and eventual death of these community members crystallized an obscured sediment of the much-discussed problem of gentrification. Although it is clear that people of diverse classes, ethnicities, races, sexualities, genders, languages, and points of view have to go somewhere when they are pushed out by a homogenized group in the so-called "cleaned up" neighborhoods in the center of a city, the dangerous conditions in which they subsequently congregate and live are not often considered. Those who are forced to leave become even more invisible, forcibly so.

For me, there is another shading that accounted for this fire being spotlighted by the newspapers and one that Luciano and I discussed earlier on the phone. It is the incredibly awful and cruel irony that those who lost their lives were what the newsrooms called "free spirits," a nomenclature whose generic use today is primarily designated for people who are enslaved, economically speaking. The repeated application of this term by news anchors, radio talk show hosts and beat writers was particularly assiduous since most of the media outlets manacled the fire victims to the biological gender scripts some were trying to escape. In most of the media's reporting, there were hes and shes and nothing beyond or in between, no they or we. With the biological error of birth following some of the victims of the fire into the beyond, their friends and survivors were angry that the news denied these "free spirits" the right to exist outside the normative project, even in death. Admitting their callousness, the media redacted these pronouns in their online articles and acknowledged the transitions some of the victims had been making into bodies and genders they were learning to be more comfortable with. Quick to change this, the media also swiftly shifted their emphasis from displays of compassion to finger pointing and investigative journalism. Who was to blame for the fire?

In retrospect, anyone looking at pictures of the Ghost Ship's interior would say a blaze was inevitable. Its ramshackle assemblage of quick-work wooden structures—rooms and nooks stuffed with old pianos and wooden dressers, sofas and baskets, prayer flags, rugs, and paper lanterns—was a labyrinthine tinderbox, a death trap with hidden exits. Many of the rooms and structures within the warehouse were illegally built and authorities had previously scrutinized the Ghost Ship for unpermitted interior construction as well as for zoning issues.

Officially, the warehouse hosted a number of artist studios, which, unofficially, was the primary residence of some of the artists who worked there. Despite the building only being zoned for commercial use, those who lived in the Ghost Ship helped to pay rent by hosting illegal parties like the one on the night of the fire. Given this information, the number of potential culprits expanded. Was the warehouse owner to blame for the fire? Or was it the main tenant? The illegal residents?

Before the criminal justice system determined in 2018 that the only two persons to be charged with involuntary manslaughter would be the main tenant Derick Almena and the tattoo artist/creative director/occasional Ghost Ship rent collector Max Harris, culpability was even flung at the organizers, the artists from 100% Silk, who booked the event at the Ghost Ship. Scorn was shown toward the label in spite of the fact that two of 100% Silk's artists, Chelsea Faith Dolan (Cherushii) and Johnny Igaz (Nackt), lost their lives in the fire. Everyone wanted to know why they would host a party in a bonfire construction. Didn't they see that an accident was highly likely if not fated?

"It's a complete tragedy," Amanda Brown, the cofounder of the label 100% Silk, told *LA Weekly* when asked in late 2016 why the artists on her label would play at a space like the Ghost Ship, "but I absolutely understand what led these people to that particular venue. We've all tried to find interesting and open-minded galleries around the country for our community to play in [but] it's incredibly hard in cities like Los Angeles and the Bay [Area] and New York to find shows for artists of this size and this type . . . there's no infrastructure for electronic music to have these safe spaces . . . [It] has nothing to do with these artists being unsafe or these artists wanting to be dangerous or to be put in dangerous situations."

As the crown of blame was passed from one devastated and anxious head to another, authorities worked to ensure that another tragedy like this would never occur. In the name of public safety, municipalities shut down buildings that did not meet previously established regulations. Simultaneously, the municipalities worked to expand and sharpen such codes, as well as to increase their scrutiny and ability to establish accountability. With the stated aim of protecting citizens and keeping them from potentially disastrous circumstances, municipalities lost in their own maze of policies and procedures veiled and/or fed into predatory market machinations that cause the displacement of those who had already been living in the margins. By forcing warehouses that serve as living/working spaces to close in cities like Oakland, Denver, Baltimore, Los Angeles, Richmond, and Fresno, communities that have limited resources started running out of alternatives, such that they have either been forced into spaces that are even more treacherous and secretive and unknown or out on the street—something the S.P.A.Z. Collective literalized by hosting a commemorative procession for the Ghost Ship victims on Oakland's boulevards in 2017. As more spaces become impossible in further cities, some may even envy the dead. At least they will be exempt from the troubles to come.

After all, where are we supposed to go?

This is where I reached a crossroads in the middle of the night while I was lying awake in some sort of dream state, typing. It was a point where I lost the vision and paused to search the internet for an apartment. *Where are we supposed to go?* It was a question that had been haunting me like a pulled muscle for more than a year. Never totally incapacitating, only inhibiting, there, I mumbled these words whenever I stared at the internet or rode my bike through the neighborhood, looking for signs. I felt the strain every time I opened the real estate portal immobilienscout24.de or read an email Melanie forwarded me for an overpriced apartment in a district we have no connection to, far from work and her family, our friends. We had been searching for an apartment for twenty months in the city that had morphed from being *"arm aber sexy"* into "Startup City #FreiheitBerlin," and we had repeatedly found nothing. With time, it began to press on me. As Melanie and I stood in line on another Sunday morning with another dozen well-groomed couples who were pre-approved applicants for an expensive apartment that was on the small side for our needs, I would look around and implore in an almost choral lamentation: *Where are we supposed to go?*

Now, late at night, I entered my own Choose Your Own Adventure story, where I tried to find a place to go. I started to speculate with my fingers on the keyboard about how migration patterns and habitation will continue to change from future market crashes, environmental disasters or war—or even just a prolongation of what we already know about the richest of the rich owning more than half of the world's wealth and increasingly more (currently, forty-two individuals possess more wealth than 3.7 billion of the world's poorest). I was hesitant to follow this fork in the road as it inevitably leads to distress and despair, which I would like to renounce, and so I will.

As an alternative, I thought I could make a diagram for the world I want to live in, something that could be filled in later. But all of the possible worlds I considered sounded more like a utopian manifesto dressed up as a novel, a fictional portrayal where social justice is real. While some small glimmer of hope in a better future has been necessary for my own survival, it currently felt defeatist to give in to the temptations of fiction. After all, there are more hazards in the world than those that are sculpted on golf courses, and there is no guarantee we wouldn't pollute this seemingly perfect place with our unaddressed negativity, the violence and complexes we've inherited and live with, deep below the surface, as if nothing else were true.

Perhaps then, I thought, I should turn away from literature and start with a lecture instead. In this lecture, I started typing, it would be useful to sketch a number of economic developments—such as the expansion of the gig economy, the increase of monopolization in online business as well as the subprime mortgage crisis in 2008—and look at how gentrification has survived in other places in other eras under different aliases. If I did look into the history of gentrification, I could begin with a quote from Karl Marx's *Capital*: "'Improvements' of towns, accompanying the increase of wealth, by the demolition of badly built quarters, the erection of palaces for banks, warehouses, &c., the widening of streets for business traffic, for the carriages of luxury, and for the introduction of tramways, &c., drive away the poor into even worse and more crowded hiding places." Or since the name Karl Marx has an air of indoctrination, I might instead open with a quote from Felix Guattari's *Three Ecologies,* from 1989: "Just as monstrous and mutant algae invade the lagoon of Venice, so our television screens are populated, saturated, by 'degenerate' images and statements. In the field of social ecology, men like Donald Trump are permitted to proliferate freely, like another species of algae, taking over entire districts of New York and Atlantic City; he 'redevelops' by raising rents, thereby driving out tens of thousands of poor families, most of whom are condemned to homelessness, becoming the equivalent of the dead fish of the environmental ecology."

In the lecture, I would then follow in the footsteps of Sarah Schulman and suggest that gentrification has negative effects on those who are pushed out of a house and a neighborhood and a city as well as on those who annex the territory. As Schulman writes, whenever everything is pasteurized, an internal replacement process alienates people from the concrete possibility of social and artistic change—something which I have experienced here in Berlin.

At this point, I wrote, I would probably break with the script of the lecture with an anecdote to warm up the public at the reading room/art space/auditorium(?) where I was delivering it, but doing this would only bring me farther away from the point I thought I was making. Afterward, I would roll up my sleeves and read another quote by Guattari from *Three Ecologies*: "At every level, individual or collective, in everyday life as well as the reinvention of democracy (concerning town planning, artistic creation, sport, etc.), it is a question in each instance of looking into what would be the dispositives of the production of subjectivity, which tends toward an individual and/or collective resingularization, rather than that of mass-media manufacture, which is synonymous with distress and despair."

This quotation is worth re-reading and I would re-read it.

"At every level, individual or collective, in everyday life as well as the reinvention of democracy (concerning town planning, artistic creation, sport, etc.), it is a question in each instance of looking into what would be the dispositives of the production of subjectivity, which tends toward an individual and/or collective resingularization, rather than that of mass-media manufacture, which is synonymous with distress and despair."

The second time around, I would let this quote stand and then not be able to not mention some anecdote that would make it clear that the distress and despair Guattari addresses is something that I and many of the people I have known in Berlin have failed to escape, either because of missing dispositives, bureaucratic hindrances or shitty conditions, like those in which the victims of the Ghost Ship fire died when they attended a "safe space" that obviously wasn't safe. It was something I had known even before then.

Suddenly, the labyrinth of the Choose Your Own Adventure story was ending.

Not with an exit, a happy end—it was moving toward the entrance.

The page with the Guattari quote, the end of the lecture, would only have one alternative at the bottom of the page, "Turn to page 162."

The top of this new page would be the end of the story.

Or what legislators at the state and federal levels thought would be the end of the story.

On this page would be the real source of the fire.

The words that aren't words, only abbreviations, codes.

The words that are almost commandments:

"2002: AB 1941 & S 2633."

In 2002, both AB 1941 (the "Anti-Rave" Bill, in the California state house) and S 2633 (the Reducing Americans' Vulnerability to Ecstasy Act, or "R.A.V.E." Act, in the U.S. Senate) aimed to ban warehouse parties, "raves," as a continuation of America's war on drugs and the crackhouse laws of the 1980s. The proposed state and federal legislation (the latter of which was pushed by Joe Biden) required electronic dance promoters to undergo a vague and burdensome permit acquisition process, whereby a promoter would have to present evidence that they were sufficiently knowledgeable about illegal drugs and drug paraphernalia before a permit's issuance.

The rave community I belonged to in the late 1990s and early 2000s considered itself lucky when these bills were shut down through our grassroots efforts, yet these proposed pieces of legislation established the foundation for 2003's Illicit Drug Anti-Proliferation Act. Although not as egregious, the Illicit Drug Anti-Proliferation Act made rave promoters liable for the actions of their patrons. Doing such was paradoxically detrimental to their safety. Previously, larger warehouse parties featured on-site medics and drug testing stations that could determine whether there were any lethal substances mixed in with the illicit drugs. After this bill passed, however, such medics and drug stations would suggest that the promoters were aware of drugs being consumed at their parties. Afraid of the legal consequences for themselves and the people inside the party, the promoters started throwing people out on the streets if they were overdosing.

Such dickish moves were the result of pigheaded legislative acts but these acts were not born in a vacuum. They were the authorities' slow response to the steady growth of unauthorized spaces over more than a decade. With its humble origins at the Full Moon parties on the beaches of San Francisco in the early 1990s, the Bay Area rave scene ballooned by the mid 1990s into countless crews and "massives" that hosted thousands upon thousands of partygoers. For years, crews like Feel Good, Funky Tekno Tribe, and Silver Pearl Records welcomed ravers to locations like 2nd & Jackson, 16th & Harrison, 111 Minna, 222 Geary, and 659 Hegenberger, the last of which was also known as the Oakland International Rave Center or "Home Base" and shared a fence with Oracle Arena.

These wild, unregulated parties bypassed the city's planning or zoning divisions, which ensured that buildings met required fire and building code and that the plumbing and electrical works were properly functioning. In the late 90s, city hall became aware of the danger such venues posed and insisted that the building owners bring the buildings up to code. When these owners were unwilling or unable to pay for the retrofitting and improved ventilation, the first death knell on nightlife in the Bay Area was a moratorium placed on New Year's Day in 2000.

And so, our exit from this Choose Your Own Adventure story only brings us to the entrance of another labyrinth. It circles into the nights after the moratorium, when raves incorporated a number of safety mechanisms, physical forms of encryption. It was another vision, or maybe a visceral memory. (Which I hope now will help illustrate what the Warriors mean by compassion from another angle, even via rave culture's failures).

I entered it.

If you attended a party at a previously undisclosed location and were given a flyer for a party a week or two later, you would find a telephone number at the bottom, the beeper of one of the organizers. You would be informed on the answering machine what record stores carried presale tickets. While the recordings early in the week were interjected with a mix of beats, the message on the day of the event was simple: go to this location across from that gas station or fast food chain between 10 PM and midnight. There, some member of the crew would size you up and ask if you already had a ticket. It didn't really matter whether you did or not, the important thing was that they didn't think you were an undercover cop. If you were in a car full of ravers, it was very unlikely that they would turn you away. But that didn't mean the encrypted message was over. You might be sent through the same procedure. You would then drive to another parking lot or gas station and undergo the same level of scrutiny. Eventually, you would slither through this labyrinth of checkpoints and arrive at the final location, maybe even on the other side of the Bay Bridge, in Oakland. The warehouse was often a shared space like the Ghost Ship. They had artist studios on the ground floor and living spaces above it. When you entered the decorated room through the warehouse door, you would be happy and a little edgy. Perhaps an undercover agent had slipped through the cracks and would disband everything, right after you took a pill of ecstasy. Or even worse: right before. Would you go to jail if you still had the drugs in your pocket? And what would you do if you didn't? If you had already taken it? Would you sit in a cell high on ecstasy? The thought always made me shudder. That would be the last thing we wanted.

What we wanted was to wear bands of aqua, pink, and antique fuchsia, to be armed with mail sleeves of plastic beads that clattered like rattlesnakes as we snaked around Jack London Square to warehouses where peaceful warriors, dressed in wigs and wings, wore pants whose cuffs were twice the size of their waist. Blowing on whistles in rhythm with the beat, we wanted to wear orange and green security vests as well as bike lights and see through visors and not be ridiculed for our ridiculous attire. Dancing in jeans and bras and white shirts that were illuminated in the black lights, we descended from a number of races and places and we were drag queens and gender benders and straight and gay and old and young. Admittedly, we were mostly young, and when we were there, we seemed much younger while we sucked on lollipops and pacifiers like children, sporting our Elmo or Teletubby backpacks. We also seemed to be from another planet or an apocalypse scenario when we wore gasmasks coated in Vic's VapoRub. Some of us also rubbed this medicinal concoction on our genitals as we danced without inhibition, playing with the music's hypnotic rhythms with our bodies, our bodies that emitted light while we explored the outer limits of our consciousness. Like the poet John Wieners writes, we wanted to be "infinite particles of the divine sun, now / worshipped in the pitch of night" and we wanted to meet friends and potential friends in a space where the day's negativity was left at the door with the bouncer. We wanted to sublimate any potential negativity through a handshake, a neon potlatch where we would exchange our beads, the "KaNDi bracelets" on our wrists and up to our elbows, in an act of PLUR, our mantra and battle cry, which stood for Peace, Love, Unity and Respect.

These were the words we lived by while the bass rearranged our cells at night, and it was the foundation of our attempt to build a compassionate community that stood in contradistinction to the competitive worldview we were forced to endure during the week. It was a disruption from the normal social relations, of the billions of individuals. We were among others and we celebrated this, but we were also, somehow, one.

This experience was presided over by the DJs, demigods or shamans, who channeled the flow of energy, sculpting seamless structures of beats faster than the embryonic human heart beats. We all mostly stood on the other side of the "decks" and were covered in sweat, intoxicated by the music and the lights in this temple of bass. In a deep state of trance and Sufi-like spinning, we threw our arms to the heavens or moved them in complex patterns with glow sticks as our eyes rolled back, inward. We mostly danced alone but there *was* kissing and close dancing and sex, yet it remained inconsequential, only interesting to those engaged in it. Just as age, gender, race, and orientation were given, unable to divide us. There was no division, no time. We were time. In it. Of it. The flow.

Naturally, the drugs made this easy. They helped us circumnavigate the blockades life set in front of us by altering our chemical settings. The most common drugs at raves were LSD, mushrooms, ketamine, weed, GHB, cocaine, methamphetamines and poppers. But most popular of all was MDMA, also known as ecstasy or X or E or Molly, which increases the release of the neurotransmitters serotonin, dopamine and norepinephrine—all things that occur naturally during activities like playing sports.

The effects of ecstasy include an increase in empathy, euphoria, and heightened sensations, and the drug does this so emphatically that even nonbelievers of this collective experience find themselves reeling and reaching out to others whom they would maybe hesitate to interact with in other spaces—which was true for so many of us, who were shy nerds. Taking ecstasy, there were times when I had difficulties discerning the difference between others and myself as we soldered ourselves together in an "E-pool" on some mattress. There were times when I could feel all of my hair follicles vibrate from the bass, an ontological shake, times when I would forget my own name, and times when I could have compassion with, well, everything.

I could demonstrate compassion for the prejudices and mistakes of others and explain them away as something they just had to experience and work through. This may have been true, but the lessons learned on drugs don't always translate into a normal waking state and the payback for synthetically eliciting this wisdom can be a bitch. Take the drug too often and the connection you feel to others is weakened then ripped out from under you when the effects wear off, only to be replaced by sluggishness and despair. While this might sound like a fair trade off—the natural conclusion of an Icarus-like climbing to new heights—the initial deliciousness of an increase of neurotransmitters from taking ecstasy is followed by a short-term decrease in them that only becomes longer. The comedown and what we all called the "cracked out" "day after" became, for me at least, a week of depression. During these days of barely being able to drag myself out of bed to attend loveless philosophy lectures or to go to work at the UC Davis Music Library, empathy would turn into antipathy, euphoria into misery, heightened sensations into concrete. This would last until the next party. And then: *Da capo! Fortissimo! Con fuoco!*

Raves weren't just about the drugs, though. For the year and a half I went to raves before experimenting with ecstasy, I was drawn to the power of sound and vision, the carnivalesque humor and chaos that implicated even wallflowers. Its power and intensity propelled me further into an alternate universe of families, tribes and communities, a large group of people seeking something counter to the "normal" order of things, an intensity invoking other intensities to form new existential configurations.

Or at least that's how it felt to me in my rave family of Wicca witches and analytic philosophers, all of whom were older and lived in the Bay Area or Sacramento Valley. In our extended crew, with its inner and concentric and overlapping circles, we shared laughter and joy and pain, and we tried to break away from what we felt was destroying us, the outside world that seemed alien, by organizing new political and social practices, new solidarities and gentleness, together with new aesthetic and analytic practices regarding the formation of minds and souls and hearts and bodies.

This crew was presided over by our matriarchs, the couple Terri and Dina. Under their guidance, we worked through the differences of pagan and analytic philosophies, seeking intersections, and fighting against strict classifications. Industrial, goth, punk, rave, and Britpop were as important to us as math and bugs and lighthouses and *Star Wars* and European cinema—and we learned from one another. Over the years, our initial dedication and softness developed into true love—and Dina was even able to work through her Neo-Nazi past through our warmth—but whenever we tried to transfer these lessons to our daily lives that had nothing to do with our crew, their incompatibility only created a binary between ravers and non-ravers. At some point, things became more fractious and we began to experience what Guattari had already warned against in the 1980s: "As experiments in the suspension of meaning they are risky, as there is the possibility of a violent deterritorialization which would destroy the assemblage of subjectification." To combat this violent deterritorialization, we tried to establish a collective and individual subjectivity that went beyond the limits of individualization with its inherent stagnation and closure, but we were unable to contain the entropic rise of a dominant subjectivity, as Guattari described it, also known as the real world.

Around 2003, when the Illicit Drug Anti-Proliferation Act was put into place, the scene started to feel like the Flying Dutchman—another ghost ship, this one famously condemned to the open seas, disallowed from ever setting anchor. As the scene moved further from the city centers, deeper into forests, wastelands and undesignated or unregulated spaces where there was nothing, no infrastructure, that could be recognized as a true venue—just a Porta Potty and decks and generators and no medics—we admitted defeat and chalked these years up to youthful excesses.

Where were we supposed to go?

Over time, we would become lawyers, real estate agents, drug counselors, city workers or California State legislators, which at first glance is ironic. We had spent a lot of time trying to figure out how to undermine exactly these institutions. But in some way, these professions could be seen as an extension of our concerns, a reminder of the times when we tried to live outside the norm—and now we wanted to change things from the inside. We mostly failed. In any case, those of us who remained true to the scene died early. The most tragic of which was when one of our beloved matriarchs, Dina, aka DJ Drag'n'fly, committed suicide in July 2017 after being alienated from us and her other loved ones for years.

As for myself, I stopped buying drum and bass records and started to agree with Aldous Huxley. Like mescaline for Huxley, ecstasy at raves could "never solve the problem: it can only pose it, apocalyptically, for those to whom it had never before presented itself. The full and final solution can be found only by those who are prepared to implement the right kind of *Weltanschauung* by means of the right kind of behavior and the right kind of constant unstrained alertness."

Although I was unable to implement the right kind of *Weltanschauung* by means of the right kind of behavior and the right kind of constant unstrained alertness, especially after all the years of damaging my brain with chemical substances, it made sense. All of those years had only been a question. A question I had learned to live and love in but which I had outgrown in its formulation. It had shrunk in the wash or become a Potemkin village, a movie set with houses that were no longer inhabitable.

This intimation remained what it was, an intimation, until in 2004 the fire of a group of homeless people got out of control and burned down Home Base, which had not been in use since the 2000 moratorium. This fire was, for me at least, the funeral pyre of an era.

End of document.

The vision was over.

* * *

Another sleepless night, another night of writing, another document. This time dated May 26, 2017 and titled inthekitchenin-venice3.docx. Melanie and I were visiting Luciano at his residency in Venice and I couldn't sleep since Luciano was snoring very, very loudly in the other room. So, I compiled my research on what I thought the Warriors meant by compassion and created a master document:

Compassion, the third core value of the Golden State Warriors, comes from the Latin and had attained three different shades of meaning by the time it was first documented in English. According to the OED, compassion can be (i) suffering together with another, participation in suffering, sympathy (1340 Ayenb. 148 Huanne on leme is zik oþer y-wonded. hou moche zorʒe heþ þe herte and grat compassion y-uelþ); (ii) the feeling or emotion when a person is moved by the suffering or distress of another, and by the desire to relieve it (c. 1340 Hampole Prose Tr. 36 Þou may thynke of synnes and of wrechidnes of thyne euencristene·· with pete and of compassione of thaym); or (iii) sorrow or grief (c. 1340 Cursor M. 23945 heading (Fairf.), Compassioun of our lauedi for þe passioun of hir sone).

But sorrow or grief is now obsolete. According to the OED, compassion is associated today with the first two entries; and this co-suffering, or feeling for another, has moved away from the word sympathy, which now carries a connotation of condolence or commiseration at a distance. The way compassion is expressed is closer to an involved form of empathy, "the power of projecting one's personality into (and so fully comprehending) the object of contemplation." And, should we follow the dictionary, it is not the case that all states and occurrences are worth empathizing with: for there to be compassion, there must be something like a broken leg, mental breakdown, or complicated divorce settlement, and the other's suffering must become to some degree one's own. Via dictionary entry number two, it is not enough to simply feel the pain, you also have to want to relieve it—compassion is active.

But then, what does any of this have to do with basketball? And why did Kerr include compassion as one of his four core values?

Compassion seems like a bad strategy if, for instance, I spend my time coddling my teammate after a missed a shot. This active form of emoting might even become doubly painful. The other team could take advantage of our pity party and score another basket on our diminished numbers. There is a way where this understanding of compassion makes sense though: a missed buzzer beater by one player is a missed buzzer beater by another. A team loses no matter who came up short or got dunked on. A team suffers together.

That would seem to fulfill the necessary and sufficient conditions for compassion according to the first entry of the dictionary. Basketball also resembles the second entry whenever I try to make up for the missed shot with tough defense on the next possession, thereby alleviating the pain of what had previously gone wrong. Kerr's inclusion of compassion as his third core value, then, would almost be trivial. It would be no different than what your average war or sports movie has to say on the subject of brotherhood and togetherness in battle.

I am not satisfied with this definition of compassion, however, since it requires a form of identification that is both too strong and too weak. It is too strong because it means I need to personally identify with the person who is suffering to be compassionate and it is too weak because it means I am only compassionate to those who are in my inner and concentric and maybe overlapping circles and not to those that are adjacent or seemingly remote. Together, they suggest we unconsciously lead our lives according to divisions, a "just us" mentality. They suggest we still hold onto the nineteenth century's bricks and mortar and are not open to becoming twenty-first century nodes. What if we saw ourselves as sites of interaction, places where emotions and thoughts pass through and not as the possessors of them? Would we still hold onto our anger and fear if we did not identify with them? If we weren't paying a mortgage to accommodate them?

Maybe a way out:

In their paper "Identity and Emergency Intervention: How Social Group Membership and Inclusiveness of Group Boundaries Shape Helping Behavior," Mark Levine and his research team at

Lancaster University explored the limitations of compassion, subtly hinting at ways in which the scope of compassion could be expanded. Inviting a group of Manchester United fans into the laboratory, the researchers asked the soccer team's devotees to answer a survey regarding their identification as fans of the Red Devils. Once the survey was finished, these fans were sent out onto the street, where the researchers had prepared a situation with someone in need. If the person on the street was wearing a Liverpool jersey, these fans would only help the person thirty-two percent of the time—Liverpool and Manchester United are rivals. In contrast, if the person in need was wearing a Manchester United jersey, the fans helped ninety-two percent of the time. This gap of exactly sixty percent in attentiveness suggests that the identification with a particular social group influences the ways in which people act compassionately.

What might need more explication would be what Levine and his team discovered when they asked Manchester United fans a series of questions about fandom and the game itself. That is, when the researchers swapped out the questions about Manchester United with questions about soccer and soccer fandom in general. When the researchers did this, the fans became less inclined to help those whom they perceived to be Man U fans (down to eighty percent) but were dramatically more willing to help those whom they perceived to be Liverpool fans (up to seventy percent). While we might speculate as to why there was a cumulative increase of twenty-six percent, the more burning question is: why were the people who weren't wearing jerseys only helped twenty-two percent of the time? What kinds of questions does a survey need to ask for the fans to show compassion to them? Do we need to broaden our notion of identification? And can we?

To do such, the dictionary would probably have to be rewritten. We would have to start at the beginning, with conjugations of beliefs. That's not a category mistake, beliefs are like verbs— the more common the belief, the more irregular are the conjugated results, they become entwined with (our) person. In the most dominant forms of Western thinking, we <u>are taught</u> that the world <u>is</u> predicated on individuality and competition. When an explanation <u>is given</u> for the capacity for selfishness and depression and violence of humans, we <u>are told</u> that our origins <u>are</u> in killer apes and that we <u>have</u> inherited this, if not through genetics, then through patriarchy. According to some feminist scholars of science and technology like Donna Haraway, the first step to changing this (note that this verb, unlike the other common verbs underlined above, is not irregular!) would be to stop believing these are our destiny; to perceive the first as a narrative, a theory, from a particular context, the late nineteenth century, and a particular set of data, the world, which is constantly changing. Elsewhere, other scholars like Anne Harrington have suggested that there are other approaches to social structures, like that of Tibetan Buddhists where compassion is understood as a guiding principle of social frameworks. According to Harrington, such societies allow for coexistence or are even predicated on it. So, let's take on those common irregular verbs. *Choose! Begin! Come!*

What I am proposing is not some utopia. It's a national park in Wyoming, for instance. This moving toward a network understanding of ecologies is something that already occurs in nature.

After wolves were reintroduced into Yellowstone to reduce the swollen deer population, badgers, geese, woodpeckers, beavers, muskrats, reptiles, mice, rabbits, weasels, red foxes, hawks, bald eagles, bugs, aspen, willow, and even the rivers have benefited from a better balance between predator and prey. In a very real way, the wolf is the friend of the river. There are objections coded as lamentations to be made regarding the loss of the fawns and I believe we can honor the deer in one breath and celebrate the gains of the red foxes in another, and know in the next breath why the wolves disappeared in the first place, they were killed off by angry farmers for agricultural business. In the next breath, I'd like you to consider that we're all in this together, that we're all the same in our difference. We'll get to this with Hannah Arendt later but for now consider the ethical dictum from the Sanskrit, the proverb *tat tvam asi*, whose translation today could be, "You're it."

In the *Upanishads*, तत्त्वमसि means you're the infinite, the eternal, the absolute, the Brahman. You are the supreme reality, the real thing, everything. Yes, that is you and it is also me. And if it is you and it is me then we are equal and identical in the infinite, eternal, absolute. And if we are always in it, no matter the circumstances, you are not another, you are me. And you are the one who is still mourning your fiancée's death six months later by isolating yourself. And you are the one who says no man is an island although you live in a huge apartment in the city alone. You don't have many friends, only a few colleagues from the lab who you sometimes watch Warriors games with, and you often eat three pieces of cake at your shifts at the cafe. Then you drink smoothie after detoxifying smoothie as your dinner and expiation. You can't believe it is over and you still need to

ease into a life without violence, but you have promised yourself to stop replaying the final voicemail and to finish what you
have started—to lose weight and be healthy again. You don't
want vengeance, but you also somehow secretly do and that is
confusing. You are much, much more than this, but you are the
one who secretly believes catastrophes are inevitable as well as
the one who has contemplated your own death down to the fin-
est details. You are definitely afraid to die, and you spend most
of your nights at bars talking at anyone who will listen to this
repetitive monologue. You don't have much time for yourself
and you don't know how to say no to your boss who asks you to
work more shifts. You never get paid overtime on those nights
you paint banks on holiday weekends, and you are afraid to ask
for it in case you get fired. It is hard to find work at your age
and it is even harder to save for your approaching retirement
in another country, a country you feel compelled to emigrate to
since you can't afford to stay in the one you whose social security system you have paid into. You are tired. And sick. And sick
and tired. You are no longer all that young and you forget to take
care of your body as you work with your younger comrades to
bring the revolution out of your minds and into the streets. You
work at the university and hate it because it is an instrument
of patriarchy, but you are always happy when it pays your travel
expenses to conferences where you congregate with others who
feel the same way. When you aren't thinking about revenge,
you are too stressed out with work to ever come into contact
with the working class you say you are defending except in taxis
from the airport. This embarrasses you immensely because it
sounds so simplistic, but you believe we must change our lives

and life in general. You have a verse by a German poet saying the same thing tattooed on your forearm, sadly with a misspelling. Everything needs to change, you say, especially what we consume and how and why we do it. For years now, you have only eaten in restaurants whose cuisine hails from countries your nation is currently bombing. "Love your enemies and bless them that persecute you" is something you often say although you are the one who persecutes anyone who doesn't look like you. Then you had the police called on you for barbequing in the park with your friends. You were arrested at home when your children were in bed because you share your name with a felon. And you were shot to death by police when you were sleeping in your car at a Taco Bell. After losing everything, you are more afraid of the police than the meth heads in the homeless encampment and you've learned that you love your estranged children more than anything. You often feel like there was some kind of mistake at your birth and you were born into a lower class than the rest of your peers and it is awkward when your friends talk about the poor and the angry and the disenfranchised in vague terms when you know how the people they are talking about wished they could live like them. You were not meant to have these parents or experiences but then you know you were. And you could do better. But you fucked up. Again. And the justice system punished you a thousand times over. It is unfair and you feel like there's something deeply wrong with our world. You are the one who wants to leave this world and its worldview behind, but you can't let go of the regret you felt when you were an asshole to everyone a week after you got back from that yoga retreat on the island. You often caught yourself saying no one could possibly understand what you had gone through but deep down you admit that that wasn't true. You feel like nothing ever changes, no matter how badly you want it. You believe change can only come from a new reconfiguration of the culture you live in and not from adopting some parts of other cultures. You are the one who left your vacation early because it made no sense to be on the other side of the world. You never returned. You found yourself at home in another country, and you became a citizen of the world, who is only able to vote in the country you haven't visited in a decade. You worked for years then suddenly stopped and dedicated yourself to your family. To your career, your fans, your writing, to me, who you are reading. You don't believe reading makes us better people, although, in another context, you said your life was changed after reading a book by an author whose name you can't remember. You can't remember if it was in *The Fire Next Time,* but you are the one who loves this quote by James Baldwin: "You think your pain and your heartbreak are unprecedented in the history of the world, but then you read. It was Dostoevsky and Dickens who taught me that the things that tormented me most were the very things that connected me with all the people who were alive, who had ever been alive. Only if we face these open wounds in ourselves can we understand them in other people." See? I told you. You are me.

And if you are me, we want this dictum to emit from our pores when we are on the court or sizing up our opponents in the unfurnished bedroom that only one of us will be panting in and sleeping in and calling home. We want to be drenched in this welcoming sweat and to be bloated with happiness as we trap past injustices behind a fresh coat of paint and vow to live our lives in these new walls without evil and hate being necessitated so that goodness can be perceived through antithesis. What I mean is, we want no ugly—and failing this, we want to love actualities and their negative capability, for we won't always be what we are, full of rashes and dandruff and warts, or what we want to be, as empty as the room we are standing in, with no against. At the very least we would like a strategy to know that you are in me, even if you are the asshole who signed the lease because you make more money, a wolf that has been reintroduced to reduce my legions. Decimating others, I do not want to forgive you—I want some orientation, away from the blindness of the mirror and the blindness of the person looking into it, who is full of anger and frustration and despair. I want to have compassion for you that is stronger than the weak and weaker than the strong definition and I do not want this to sound naïve or stupid. I want to remember a question from the Situationists—"To what extent can we freely build the framework for a social life in which we might be guided by our aspirations and not our instincts?"—and I want to answer "100%." This is not some utopian fantasy, I swear. There are models we can follow where people work toward their aspirations and are not ruled by the instincts they've inherited from our "just us" worldview. The Warriors under Kerr's direction are one such model and it is their understanding of compassion that makes this possible.

Not that Coach Kerr is opposed to the dictionary.

Kerr's alignment with the OED's first definition of compassion was on full display when he paid his condolences to the victims of the Ghost Ship fire in a pregame presser the day after the fire (I realized as I read my notes from Venice that I had been much busier with Josh and the fire than I had thought). Kerr expressed his sympathy and the sympathy of the whole organization before moving on "to basketball matters, the stuff that doesn't matter."

Kerr's small speech and expression of compassion was not some platitude—together with the other two major sports teams that were based in Oakland at the time, the Raiders and the Athletics, the Warriors organization raised more than $250,000 for the victims of the fire. This donation was followed by that of the Warriors players and coaching staff who pooled together another $75,000.

Moving down another scale in dimension to the individual, Stephen Curry auctioned off two pairs of his signature shoes to raise funds for the victims as well. These custom versions of Curry's Under Armour sneakers were designed by an Oakland artist and came in two iterations: the black low-top pregame shoes that had "Ghost Ship" written in yellow, orange, red, and blue graffiti on each shoe, and the white high-top game shoes that read "Oakland" on the left foot and "Strong" on the right in yellow and blue on the shoes' uppers.

Together, these two pairs of shoes that Curry wore on December 15, 2016, in the Warriors' home game against the New York Knicks (the same night that Kerr honored Craig Sager with a moment of joy instead of silence), raised more than $45,000 for the victims of the fire. As such, those who lost their lives made their presence felt on the court as well.

(I looked up the shoes again: all of the initials of the Ghost Ship victims were on the heels of both pairs of shoes and in both cases, Donna's were near the cuboid bone—which, Wikipedia tells me, is called the *Würfelbein*, the dice-leg, in German. It's an upsetting translation. It's like we're always standing on luck.)

* * *

In the game of basketball, the Warriors express their dedication to compassion by belonging to a "five-man connection" that is established on offense by sharing the ball with one another. Never stagnant, they are constantly screening for one another and passing to one another, creating a network of possibilities with their bodies in motion. The Warriors players are like nodes, sites of interaction. Although this does not mean each and every player is indistinguishable, it still creates an environment in which everyone is involved and the players feel connected. This then forces the defense of the other team to communicate properly on possessions that involve three or four or five of the Warriors players more often than one on one or two on two as is common with other teams.

An illustration from the 2016–17 season: Draymond Green has the ball at the top of the key then passes it to Kevin Durant who is posting up on the left-hand side. With no shot there, he passes it back to Draymond who has drifted back behind the three-point line. He finds Klay Thompson coming off a screen at the left wing and when he catches the ball he passes to Zaza Pachulia at the elbow. Zaza drops the ball between his legs into the hands of Steph Curry, who has been zigging and zagging through a series of cuts and screens, and then finally close to the corner on the same side as Zaza. Steph fakes a shot, his defender flies by, and he reloads. When the ball goes through the net and Steph performs an awkward celebration from his repertoire, they run back to the other side of the court and get ready for their defensive assignments, where their switches and help and individual defense are so fluid and in synch that it seems totally unspectacular. And, in a way, Kerr's version of compassion is unspectacular.

Speaking with the Positive Coaching Alliance, Coach Kerr expressed it like this: "It's really important for the team to have compassion for each other. Every player is different. Michael Jordan is so much better than the rest of the team that he may not see the game the way I did for example as the eighth man on the Bulls . . . Compassion between team members is critical. Understanding that everybody has different pressures on them but acknowledging that in a daily manner really establishes a good tone, a good routine, a good environment to work in."

If I were to create a new definition for the dictionary that would sum up all of this, I would say that compassion has to do with nurturing your ecology. By nurturing an ecology, I mean creating and maintaining an environment that is habitable for everyone as well as respecting the needs and abilities of others in an environment that allows for difference, while also realizing that we're all interconnected—and that includes non-human actors. (I note: this is something we did as ravers.) As Kerr told *The Athletic*, "I believe in the power of the group."

But what is the group? Is it the team? Or does it extend even further? I believe that it can extend further and that it does and that Kerr would not disagree—his acts of compassion to the Ghost Ship fire victims and survivors is but one example of him looking beyond the team. In any case, it is also important that the group believes in the power of the group, they have to understand The Secret, they have to say, "WE BELIEVE." And some of the Warriors would have to learn it.

To learn—another common irregular verb. Irregular because

it is circuitous, if not arduous, in that learning often involves unlearning, a process of overcoming; and common because there is no other way than through. For, although the above sections might give the impression that the saintly Warriors immediately recognized the value of abandoning their egos for the glory of something greater, the apocryphal section, the appendix, would show that this did not happen by coincidence or divine intervention. They would have to make The Choice.

Unlike the Apostle Paul's immediate conversion, Andre Iguodala needed convincing to go to the second string, and once he was there, he wasn't very happy at first. Iguodala is the kind of player that other coaches would encourage to be the team's biggest aggressor and he is fully capable of being the No. 1 option on offense—and he would be on many of the twenty-nine other teams. But he decided to buy in to the Warriors' ideas. And, as the Warriors' assistant coach Mike Brown said, "That's the foundation of this organization."

Another player that had trouble adapting to the principles that Kerr was establishing is Draymond Green, the "emotional leader of the team," who initially found the "Strength in Numbers" concept to be "corny." Complicated and tortuous, Green's acceptance of Kerr's four core values has been under scrutiny continuously, even, allegedly, from the team.

As Ethan Strauss reported in his ESPN story "Golden State's Draymond Green Problem," Kerr is said to have been directly addressing Green with the importance of compassion in his speech about the Warriors' four core values before the game in Phoenix in the early days of the 2015–16 season. This makes sense to anyone who has watched Green's at times fervent and/or repellant behavior on the court, where he seems to be the domineering wolf unleashed on the legions of other teams. Green is often seen, like Saul before becoming Paul, as "breathing out threatening and slaughter," collecting technical fouls like others do stamps or pogs. He is the overbearing player who for many years had screamed "and-1" at the refs after every failed layup as if he were met with some heinous injustice for his failing to convert a simple basket. He is best known to his detractors for swinging at LeBron James' nether regions in Game 4 of the 2016 NBA Finals after James threw him to the ground and stepped over him. As a consequence of Draymond's swipe at James and his previous history of kicking other players in the nards, the league decided a day after Game 4 that Green would have to be suspended for Game 5 of the Finals—which, if you're a Warriors apologist, was the real reason they lost the championship that year.

Often overzealous, Draymond has seemed like a liability to the team. During the "BANG! BANG! OH WHAT A SHOT FROM CURRY" Game, the reporters even expressed their dismay about Draymond, who had been screaming "I am not a robot!" during halftime in Oklahoma City and reportedly even tried to fight Coach Kerr. But, like all of us, Green is full of contradictions and he has become a scapegoat for all of the Warriors' problems (even though he causes only some). No one seems to remember that he was a finalist for the NBA Cares Community Assist award for the 2015–16 season for his active role in the #Leanintogether public awareness campaign focused on the important role men play in reaching gender equality, as well as his position on the advisory board of the RISE organization to help advance race relations. That year, Green also participated in the anti-bullying campaign

Not On Our Ground, was the spokesperson of the Warrior's Go Green platform, which informed spectators on how to be more ecological, or "green," at home, and worked with his teammates and 3,000 season ticket holders to deliver 20,000 lunch bags to school children in need. In other words, Green has nurtured his ecology on a public level at least.

As far as basketball goes, Kerr has repeatedly told reporters whenever a negative portrait of Green is painted by the media that he's a valuable part of the team and well loved by his teammates and management. Joe Lacob, for example, wore his jersey for the game Green was suspended in the 2016 NBA Finals and Bob Myers watched the game with Green next door at the Oakland A's venue, the Oakland Coliseum. Both of them know that Green is integral to the Warriors' success. The head coach does as well. "It's hard to describe what he does," Kerr has said, "but he's a perfect modern-day NBA player."

Although Green plays power forward, a position traditionally operating from the post and thus close to the basket, Green often acts as the playmaker in Golden State's positionless offense. He is capable of taking the ball to the rim after a pick and roll with Stephen Curry or finding the open man when the defense collapses on him, whether that be a lob to a rolling player or a skip pass to the three-point line. He's an elite passer who always has his head up, looking to make plays for others, but can also attack gaps in the defense before it recovers. And on defense, he is the ultimate coordinator of his teammates' positioning, who is also capable of closing out on a three-point shooter by running from under the basket and entering lightspeed to block the shot of the opponent. Given his amazing passes, ridiculous complaining, unparalleled efforts, and monster showboating, Strauss has described Green's approach to the game as "a revolution. It's an aggressive, American brashness mixed with an egalitarian, European insistence on moving the ball." Green fits the on-court interpretation of nurturing your ecology and, as the plays detailed in this book show, he is always in the center of everything.

Nothing shows his understanding of nurturing your ecology as much as his relationship to the triple-double. A triple-double is achieved when a player exceeds a double-digit number in three of the five statistical categories—points, rebounds, assists, blocks, or steals. On paper, a triple-double signifies a complete game, the ability to be a driving force on offense and defense as well as the ability to recognize other teammates through passing. A triple-double is thus a perfect balance between selflessness and selfishness. It signifies that a player is willing to do whatever it takes to win the game and enter something new. Traditionally, the triple-double has been held in high regard because it suggests that the player understands The Secret.

But it can backfire and even suggest its opposite.

The night after Kerr visited the Warriors to remind them of his four core values, the team was playing against the Phoenix Suns in the seventeenth game of the 2015–16 season. The Warriors had won every contest before and with a little more than four minutes left in the game against the Suns, Green fouled one of the Suns' players. Interim head coach Luke Walton pulled Green out of the game. An animated discussion ensued between the coach and the player, with Green begging to be let back in. Walton conceded. After Ian Clark missed a layup, Green rebounded the ball and laid it in. In the next possession, he intentionally fouled a Suns' player then walked back to the bench at ease. He had just achieved his goal, a triple-double.

Two months later, Kerr's back was healthy enough to be on the sidelines and Green had ten points, ten boards, and six assists at the end of the second quarter in a game against the Philadelphia 76ers. Kerr reportedly informed Green that if he's hoping for a triple-double against what was then the worst team in the league (a team that was still tanking), it would have to come in the third quarter. He no longer wanted Green to keep wasting his time playing garbage minutes for stats. Green agreed in principle, though not with Kerr's intent. On the first play of the second half, Green got the ball and had an open lane to the rim, but he chose instead to set a screen for Klay Thompson and pass him the ball. This resulted in a turnover and this turnover was followed by many others. Green committed seven turnovers in all, helping to allow a nineteen-point fourth quarter lead be erased. Luckily, in the last two-tenths of a second, he dished the ball to Harrison Barnes who made the winning basket, giving Green his ninth assist and, with it, another victory toward the team's historical season of seventy-three wins. After the game, Green admitted he was playing a "selfishly unselfish game" and that the Warriors deserved to lose "because that's what happens when you mess around with the game and the ball." That season, Green would tally thirteen triple-doubles, some more forced than others, but the Warriors were always undefeated when he achieved this goal.

A year later, after Green was suspended for Game 5 of the 2016 NBA Finals, and after the Warriors lost the Finals to the Cleveland Cavaliers, something changed in the way Green approached the game. Not only would he be named Defensive Player of the Year, but he also stopped hunting for triple-doubles. Not that he didn't get them—indeed his fourth of five triple-doubles was one of the most remarkable stat lines in NBA history: he had twelve rebounds, ten assists, and ten steals, along with just four points. It was the first time that a triple-double had ever been recorded with less than ten points.

But for me, this wasn't Green's most remarkable performance of the season. That came on April 2, 2017. Green was one basket away from totaling a triple-double and there was one minute left in the game. Green had the ball and was given the go-ahead to shoot but was suddenly double-teamed. He saw that the Warriors' center JaVale McGee was open and threw him an alley-oop. It looked like his opportunity was gone, there was little time in the game, the window seemed to close. Then, two Warriors' possessions later, he brought the ball up the court and passed it to Matt Barnes on the wing. When Green's man hedged off him, Barnes passed the ball back to Green and he nailed a three, tallying his fifth and final triple-double of the season. What is noteworthy here is that this play was not forced. The ball came to him and he made the basket. According to the Warriors' courtside reporter at the time, Ros Gold-Onwunde, Green knew that he was close to a triple-double but he said, "I just want to play the right way. There'll be other chances and, if not, I've had a triple-double before. I'll be OK. It's more important for the team to see that." As such, Green seemed to have learned the lesson of the Warriors' assistant coach Jarron Collins: "Play the right way and the show will happen."

(In his memoir, Andre Iguodala would say something similar:

"And when I became a player [for the Warriors], that respect for the game was everywhere. Not just in the building [i.e. the fans], but in the organization, and especially in the coaching. It was like a kind of faith, a very fundamental belief that by truly focusing on the game, on executing it at a high level, on treating each player as an adult, and as a professional, then the rest would take care of itself.")

By playing the right way, Green has nurtured his ecology and has aligned himself with Guattari's proposal that revolutionary practices "must not be exclusively concerned with visible relations of force on a grand scale, but will also take into account molecular domains of sensibility, intelligence, and desire." He has mastered these "molecular domains," which are known as "intangibles" in the world of sports, attributes or behavior an athlete displays that have nothing to do with physical prowess. As the Warriors' guard Shaun Livingston put it, "It's all the little things [Green] does that win championships."

My notes from May 2017 end here.

As I read this now, late in the afternoon on February 10, 2018, the day after Luciano and I talked on the phone about life and Josh, I'm listening to the album *Silk to Dry the Tears*, which 100% Silk released yesterday to honor the Ghost Ship victims in "the spirit of inclusion, endurance, and empathy." It's a beautiful tribute, and while I've been listening to the first couple of tracks and reading through these different documents, I've realized that much of what's been said above could be summed up by the sports cliché "great players make other players better." But at the same time, I know that this cliché isn't enough. There are too many counterexamples. What is needed in addition is a system wherein all of the players can feel empowered to be great themselves—and to help one another. By placing the good of the team above your personal ambitions, you learn how dependent we all are on one another. None of us are acting in a void and all of our actions influence countless others. We need to be able to really care about other people and to sacrifice for them, which requires discipline and awareness and effort. We need to realize how similar we are though different. In other words, PLUR. Without the drugs. For the sake of maintaining the right *Weltanschauung*, we cannot lose touch with the world. We must nurture our ecologies at all times. Today, entrenched in my memories and thoughts about the rave scene and Dina and Donna in particular, this feels important to stress. As Cornell West writes, "Either we learn a new language of empathy and compassion or the fire this time will consume us all." Which is also why, I thought, I was so upset about the guy in the bookstore and also Josh.

Octo Octa's track "Not Sure What to Do (Variation Zoning 4)" on *Silk to Dry the Tears* is now playing.

I just texted Luciano for Josh's number and he answered immediately.

He wouldn't recommend getting in touch with his other best friend. Things have taken a turn for the worse. The last time Luciano spoke to him, Josh was trying to convince him to believe in conspiracy theories like Pizzagate. He probably wouldn't want to know that anyone was thinking about him—it would only make him more paranoid.

That's OK. I don't want to be invasive or say anything that comes across as flat, plastic, or cold. Sometimes it's better to stay away from the sidelines. I'm learning that to nurture your ecology is complicated and that it can never be reduced to simplistic "good intentions." It may not be much, but it's a start.

Beginning, Again

Basketball is a bridge that can carry you from one state to another but it is also the flowing river and the vehicle you control, until invisible black ice derails you, causing your vehicle, your body, to plummet or go up in smoke. (Cross this out, start again.)

Basketball is a jackhammer—pounding away at sedimentation—as well as a confessional—in the game you can release your innermost feelings and frustrations in a safe space, a home for belief, that prepares you for the apocalypse, the Second Coming. (Cross this out, start again.)

Basketball is a game, a holy place where you can just focus on what you're doing: dribbling, moving, guarding, shooting. And if you're really locked in, you can counter everything that's presented to you with new moves. And then, when you hit the game winner in your driveway or at the playground or in the gym and you wear laurel wreaths on your sweaty head, basketball is a hit of ecstasy, you get high from getting it together in action. (Cross this out, start again.)

Basketball is also a laboratory to try out new things, a game of chess to test your strategy, and at times a legislative chamber or casino floor where you can get lucky—but most importantly, it's a sanctuary featuring an altar of dreams, dreams that are dead and dying, dreams that are immortal. Because we will never be as good as Stephen Curry, no matter how hard we try. We are mere mortals and not demi-gods. There's no way to escape it. (Cross this out, start again.) Basketball is much more than this, but it is also totally humiliating.

In any given play, you might get hit with a back screen, leaving you bottled up and confused. Or, you might get switched onto a bigger opponent who will feast on your smaller frame, backing you down in the paint, dunking all over your face. There's not a lot you can do to stop this, and most of your teammates will just shrug their shoulders as a consolation. But what they won't accept is when you stop paying attention. You should roll to the basket when you set a pick in the pick-and-roll. When you forget to perform half of the name of the play and you drift out to the elbow, your teammate will throw the ball to where they expected you to be, to where you should be, and the ball might soar out of bounds or land in your opponent's hands.

Afterward, your teammate might start clapping. Not out of praise, but out of anger. *Clap clap clap clap.* I have heard these four hard handclaps countless times when I've turned the ball over on a pass I had no business throwing. Or when my opponent bounced the ball between my spread legs—when I got "nutmegged." I have stood, flatfooted and caught in a web of reflections about my foot positioning and lateral movement, as my opponent then converted a layup. I have tried to blame this lack of movement on my inhibited flexibility due to my back surgery but most often my teammates don't want to hear it. They just want me to pay attention. And when I hear these four claps again, it can be rather discouraging, if not downright embarrassing.

But then: "Basketball is about getting embarrassed."

This is an encouraging statement I would be willing to accept if this Pythian wisdom had been intended to make weekend warriors like me feel better about their failures. Sadly, it wasn't. These words were a reminder by Kevin Durant that effort is everything and that you should never give up on a play—either through carelessness or inability or bad positioning or lack of commitment.

You are *supposed* to get embarrassed when you play basketball, especially professionally. You cannot worry about "getting put on a poster," you have to challenge the dunk attempt of your opponent. We must give our full effort and despise the fear of failure. We must make a vow with ourselves to never relinquish our lives to mere contingencies, imagined inevitabilities. We must be willing to be humiliated while renouncing the word humiliation. We have to stay in the game.

And, perhaps surprisingly, the same goes for those of us watching.

Durant made a point of this when he joined Bill Simmons on his podcast on April 14, 2018. According to Durant, we viewers cannot let ourselves succumb to distractions like the thousands of "blog boys" who endlessly quantify basketball with a "flawed" set of metrics. The Blog Boys who prefer to discuss effective field goal percentage or create memes where centers dance to the stars as they get crossed over by Curry to then post them for karma points on r/nba. What's more important, Durant said, is to be present. Why? Because watching basketball has the potential to be a transformative experience that goes beyond any meme or potential number crunching. Watching the game can be as refreshing as a daylong hike from Delphi to the Corycian Cave, a former place of refuge during foreign invasions. Watching basketball, you can feel galvanized, excited, tingly. You might even feel inspired. Not necessarily divinely—though perhaps also. You can see what could happen if you dedicate your life to what's important to you. By doing such, basketball lifts you up. Basketball raises your spirits. Or, as Durant said in his 2014 MVP speech, "Basketball is just a platform for me to inspire people."

Watching Durant perform in all of the 256 games he played in during the three seasons he was with the Golden State Warriors, I can attest to being inspired by his crossovers and fade-away jumpers. There is an elegance to his game that now touches my aesthetic sensibility much more than contemporary forms of art and poetry that express disdain for the audience or that purposefully remain obfuscating. It has taken years for me to realize that an artist does not need to be "challenging," i.e. purposefully difficult and/or confrontational. Instead, an artist can elevate higher by digging deeper, into and beyond the self, while everyone holds their breath, in the stands, together.

Basketball, then, is about creating an experience. And by extension, Durant suggests that basketball is about being in the world. But it isn't so simple. As we know, Pythian riddles never are. Basketball is also its opposite. Just listen to Coach Kerr: "For most of us who play this game or coach this game, this is kind of our refuge, being able to play, being able to immerse yourself in the game."

This, of course, is a paradox. The Blog Boys will get their meme machines ready and caption a photo of the black hole *Powehi*—whose name means the "embellished dark source of unending creation"—with "Basketball is about being in the world and escaping it." Yet, like most paradoxes that frustrate reason, this Pythian meme also contains a multitude of truths.

Durant expressed it best. After losing to the Warriors in the 2016 Western Conference finals, Durant, who then played for the Oklahoma City Thunder, told reporters there are "so many emotions we try to bottle in, and also let out when we're on the floor. And I think the guys [on the Thunder] did a good job of using basketball as a refuge, just letting it out and letting that be a shield for everything and just being yourself when you're out here on the floor."

According to that logic, basketball can provide a lens to look at yourself—basketball is a microscope or telescope to find what's hidden in plain view. Basketball also allows you to establish a link with the person you really are. Or, more emphatically, as the ex-player cum philosopher cum theologian cum shaman, Onaje X.O. Woodbine, writes in *Black Gods of the Asphalt*, the game can offer those society normally persecutes or ignores a place to gain recognition: "In the flow of the game we could discover a feeling of worth the larger society would not afford us."

One of the great dramas in life is this doesn't last forever. Though different, I knew this. Every time I dented the garage door while practicing fadeaways or tore pieces of sheetrock out of my bedroom wall when I dunked on my Nerf backboard, I had to face the fact that life doesn't like to be shut out for too long.

Even if you play an excellent game without mistakes, you

might anger your uncle, who outweighs you. Fighting for his pride, this uncle might "accidentally" elbow your fourteen-year-old face as you imitate Michael Jordan on a reverse layup in the driveway. If he does and your tongue is stuck out, you might almost bite right through it. Coming from humble beginnings means a trip to the hospital is out of the question unless a bone has become visible, or worse. This is something you would like to avoid anyway. The last time you went to the down-market medical center from a basketball injury—when you developed tendonitis in your young knees and could no longer walk or bend them—you were made to feel the incredible guilt of shouldering your family with medical debt. Back then, you may have only landed awkwardly while trying to save the ball from grazing your father's newly reseeded lawn but the cost of all the braces and lengthy treatments for tendonitis in both knees was not easily forgotten. So, in moments like these, you hope your tongue will stop bleeding. When it does, you swallow your grace with meal after meal of cinnamon applesauce and pray for the day you can eat solids again. Meanwhile, you keep playing.

Seeing sports as a sanctuary has been critical not only for aspiring athletes trying to make their way in and through the world but also for theorists who wish to delineate the function of athletics. The first, most fundamental premise of both jocks and nerds is that sports "always appear to be at a distance from the interests and strategies that make up our everyday world," as the literary scholar Hans Ulrich Gumbrecht has written. With the ball in our hands, the day's dentist appointment, spreadsheets, traffic, and unanswered introspections seem to vanish. We focus solely on our movements, our teammates, opponents, the present, as we catch the ball then square our shoulders and hips before launching up for a jump shot within an eternity of seconds. Often, we feel as if we are part of something greater than the concerns of our wrinkled organs and we love it. We love it for providing solace from the pressures of our work and social obligations, for suspending the weight of what equips our existence with meaning; our relationships, beliefs, and desires, out of which our lives are assembled.

This does not mean the presence dimension is without meaning. In it, we experience events and phenomena that have an impact on our bodies and senses. Through training, repetition, and playing, our bodies and sensory apparatus learn ways of moving, of perceiving, of being, and this gives us meaning both on and off the court. As Gumbrecht suggests, "Knowledge is not exclusively conceptual."

Perhaps surprisingly, Gumbrecht does not limit sport's sense of presence to those who have sweat pooling on the smalls of their backs either. Like Durant, Gumbrecht pushes further in his *In Praise of Athletic Beauty* and argues we are also in the presence dimension when we spectate. Until the final horn blows, players, coaches, announcers, and viewers are all snuggled up in the present. Totally immersed in the moment, we are inseparable from what we are doing. We are aware only of what's happening, the present, as we hold our breath when the ball leaves Stephen Curry's hands, and we are ecstatic—or devastated—when it touches nothing but net. "This kind of experience," Phil Jackson writes, "happens all the time on the basketball floor; that's why the game is so intoxicating."

That's also why, to go back to the beginning, all those

Portland Trail Blazers fans were incensed during the game against the Warriors on April 14, 2010. The fans were livid that this precious realm could be litigated against and suspended, that Don Nelson barricaded them from their hard-earned entry to presence with his exegesis. Thoughts like these lead Gumbrecht to hypothesize further that the real function of sports, the reason the billion-dollar industries of athletic spectacles are so damned important today, is that they provide us with a key to the door of presence in a society that has lost most other points of entry: "A scarcity of presence components in everyday life may produce an overwhelmingly strong desire to see the world from an angle of presence. For what we most desire is almost always the hardest to obtain."

In my own life, this sounds about right. I find it difficult to get to this realm of presence when there are bills to pay, calls to make, annoying customers, and lines at the grocery store. There is the continual frustration in not feeling appreciated by my boss at the bookstore and my embarrassment for not letting it go when I drag on about it over dinner with Melanie. And there are moments where I seek refuge from the weight of worrying about my mother by reverting to old patterns of behavior that I had developed during the years of my anxiety-riddled depression, such as smoking. Whenever I am able to put aside life's concerns in a healthy way, though, I am always very grateful. I feel my shoulders slacken, my jaw unclench, and a sense of calm and focus. Nowadays, after shooting hoops or meditating, I perceive a distance between myself and my daily preoccupations. This distance does not erase them. It only disallows them from affecting me as violently as before.

This may seem to corroborate the fundamental premise of jocks and nerds, but it subtly yet irrevocably modifies the refuge into a thoroughfare. The world is not irrelevant; it is something I am in and something I can change my behavior in relation to. With practice, the power on the court can bleed into all other activities. I can find the same level of presence in the bookstore or U-Bahn, and this might be as mundane as simply being there and not busying myself with my phone or worrying about something in the past or the future. I can lock in.

I doubt however that life can be totally shut out or that we should let it. No matter how enraptured I may be watching a game on Sunday, there's still the laundry—and I know it. Commercial breaks or timeouts remind me of every unanswered email, and I don't instantly forget them when the game starts up again. It seems to me there is a way to see the realms of presence and meaning as islands in an archipelago. And I would like to think that when the tide of hyperrationalization is out we can take them for what they are, connected by a sandbar, which is only invisible because of a lack of focus that succumbs to the onslaught of so-called diversions, self-absorbed anxieties and "chores."

Nevertheless, the notion of sports as a refuge is pervasive and very convincing. When I was in college, my father would often lecture me before the family functions I felt obligated to attend about what I was allowed to discuss with my extended relatives. Philosophy, religion, literature, and politics were out, and since I hadn't seen the latest blockbusters, that left only sports. "Just stick to sports," he'd say, "and none of that other bullshit." Sports represented a space where we could all come together.

Sports were the great equalizer where glaziers, painting contractors, 911 operators, students, and the disabled were all in the same league. Sports were an analogue for living democratically, horizontal coexistence. We could do away with what disbanded us and unite in the presence of the seventh inning. The problem with this wishful thinking is that the women in our families were never welcome to watch the games. They were laughed at for not understanding the rules or for mixing up the names of players and teams. Even worse, they were told to shut up during the broadcast. The problem, in essence, has to do with exclusion, and, by extension, with the misconception that presence should exclude meaning.

Still, I subscribed to this reasoning. Not wanting to make these obligatory visits feel longer than they already did by sitting in the corner, glumly sipping on some beverage, I would study the box scores, standings, trades, playoff pictures, and draft prospects for football and baseball before Thanksgiving, Christmas, or family reunions in the summer. And so, if my uncles or cousins ever started slinging mud at their wives or doctors or employees or bosses, I would praise the Oakland Raiders or Oakland Athletics—none of them liked basketball—and the day's pigment would change from thunderclouds to a sunset. My family would temporarily forget I was a "pinko" and would agree with my assessment of the team or educate me about the intricacies I was missing.

Just as hungry for harmony and frightened by discord as my father, I was always happy when we talked about the pigskin and got lost in numbers. My Republican, Mormon-converted, extended family would forget I was the only cousin out of more than a dozen getting a "liberal" education when we discussed field goal percentage rates and the best left-handed closers. These facts and statistics suspended time and judgment as good as any Hail Mary—or perhaps even better.

Watching the games also had an air of unpredictability that could unlace tightly wrapped beliefs. Certain plays could facilitate foul smelling bigotry to be aired in heated moments without thinking. On more than one occasion, an opponent outran or outwitted a Raider and some member of my extended family yelled, "Get that nigger," and I lost it.

Could they really be so ignorant?

Were they really such fucking pigs?

If it was one of my uncles or cousins who said this and not my father, he would do his best to calm me.

I would get ready to leave as the announcers washed over the awkwardness.

They didn't mean it like that, they'd say.

Didn't I know how to take a joke?

Sadly, this is not a rarity. Athletes and sports fans all over the world show where they stand, then and there, in this realm of presence and our access to it is shaped by past experiences, future aspirations and beliefs—that is, meaning. During that pickup game with my uncle, for instance, both of us were venting old grievances. It was a classical matchup between a bully and a nerd, and we were fighting within and against these categories as much as with one another. Possessed by an ancient yet adolescent animosity toward a tyrant who always exhibited his greatness by brutishly throwing his weight around, I wanted to prove that my interest in intellectual pursuits would not limit my physical performance. More, I wanted to prove these interests would enhance my ability, even if only by psychologically discombobulating my opponent when I called a crossover, left-side flip bank shot then sank it—a tactic I had learned from reading stories about Larry Bird.

When my uncle's elbow connected with my face and I christened him an asshole and he pushed me into the Ponderosa pine tree on the lawn next to our driveway on Warr Road, it was a momentary consummation of his rage toward a life of never feeling like he was good enough, a frustration that explained why he always enjoyed squashing my cousins and me in horseshoes, ping-pong, or Monopoly. Later that day, he would begrudgingly apologize for getting carried away in the game and I would only accept his stated sense of regret in my heart after my father revealed his brother was having a hard time coping with the physical and mental consequences of his recently diagnosed multiple sclerosis. I was still angry hours later when everyone was feasting on ribs and corn and I had to gum apple purée, but I realized my uncle's condition must not be easy for him. It was then that I had an embryonic hunch of the impossibility of banishing the world from the four corners of the court.

Without yet being fully aware of it, that day demonstrated that even if we believe the interests and strategies making up our everyday world are provisionally suspended while watching or playing sports, we are just what we are at that moment, and that can be ugly. This is one reason why many intellectuals are allergic to sports and condemn its adrenaline-fueled violence. Characterizing sports as a mere distraction, some intellectuals have even suggested sports have replaced religion as the opiate for the masses. I find this hard to believe since eighty-four percent of the world population still belongs to some creed, and I can't compute someone stomping through the face of a rival fan while being high on heroin. If anything, sports and sports fandom would have to be more like PCP; a dissociative drug that induces a false sense of detachment from the world as well as exaggerated strength and aggression.

Case number 24,369,047: in the summer of 2016, videos surfaced of clashes between English and Russian soccer hooligans before the European Cup began in France. As these hooligans ripped through Marseille's city center, they did their best to destroy one another with bottles, fists, iron bars, and café chairs. Many people were injured in the battles as well as in others in Lille, Paris, Nice, Saint-Étienne, and Lyon. Countless arrests were made, and bans were placed on alleged hooligan bosses from entering the stadiums or country, yet this reaction by the authorities was only a band-aid on a seismic rip. According to *The Economist*, the tournament's organizers even expected violence, except, as always, "not like this."

The xenophobic violence marring the European Cup was in abundance even outside of France. Here in Germany, it happened, in part, with words. The far-right politician Alexander Gauland from the right-wing populist party AfD (*Alternative für Deutschland*) intimated that the West Berlin native Jérôme Boateng may be a great soccer player, but he wasn't the kind of person you would want as a neighbor. When the news agency *Der Spiegel* gave Gauland space to clarify his remarks about the heavily tattooed, deeply religious and good-natured Boateng, Gauland doubled down instead of folding. Boateng, whose father is from Ghana and mother from Germany, wasn't the only problem according to Gauland. Also on the German team was Mesut Özil, who is a third-generation Turkish-German. This wasn't necessarily a problem for Gauland—the website *Politically Incorrect* has indicated that more than a third of AfD voters have a *Migrationshintergrund* (migration background) and thus Gauland had to be careful not to insult a considerable portion of his constituency. What was truly despicable for Gauland was that Özil is a practicing Muslim. How dare he visit Mecca when he's supposed to be a role model for children! In this conversation, Gauland let it all hang out: the German team wasn't even German anymore. They were all just a bunch of rich foreigners looking to grab some cash. It was time, he believed, for Germany and its football team to become German again.

I know, it's distressing. It's distressing that these forms of nationalism and racism are even put on parade during major sporting competitions and that it is perfectly acceptable to indulge in. Having moved to Berlin in 2005, I witnessed this here in the *Land der Dichter und Denker* (Land of Poets and Thinkers) when Germany hosted the World Cup in 2006. Though open displays of patriotism had been problematized for generations after the Second World War, in 2006 the German flag was like pollen. It drifted from balcony to billboard to t-shirt to decal to face paint to—everything was covered.

At the time, there was an intense debate in the media about the legitimacy of such outright forms of patriotism given the country's condemnable history of genocide, but the consensus seemed to be it was good for young Germans, three or four generations removed from the atrocities of the previous century, to get over the guilt trip they had inherited. They should feel free to support their national soccer team like the teenagers they were. That year, national pride was cautious and awkward and nevertheless insidious. Racial and national stereotypes were slowly flaunted, laughed at, and agreed upon. By the time of the World Cup final, Italians were all lazy spaghettis, the French, dandies more concerned with their appearances—and this wasn't the worst of what I experienced. When Zinedine Zidane headbutted Marco Materazzi in overtime in the World Cup final, someone at the viewing party Grace and I stumbled onto blurted out that only a ruffian immigrant would end his career in such a base fashion.

Zidane's final act as a footballer was certainly shocking and it has never stopped dividing opinions. While news agencies like *Slate* called the head butt a "scene from a French gangster flick" and then detailed Zidane's history of dirty plays, others have justified Zidane's reaction once lip-readers deciphered the racist insults of Materazzi. Some artists have gone further and been inspired by Zidane's bravery. Immortalized, for instance, as a bronze sculpture by the artist Adel Abdessemed (who described the head butt as "an act of freedom"), the game and the head butt were also the focal point of the essay "Zidane's Melancholy" by the writer Jean-Philippe Toussaint. In this essay, Toussaint eulogizes Zidane's sense of presence—Zidane "experienced with heartrending intensity the feeling of simply being there, in the Olympic Stadium in Berlin, at that precise moment, the evening of the World Cup final." Interesting here is that Toussaint also confirms Gumbrecht's hypothesis that spectators are in the same dimension of presence as the athletes. Toussaint details his own relation to the present as a spectator and identifies some version of himself, the narrator, with the football hero, going even so far as to suggest, "Zidane's melancholy is my melancholy, I know, I've fed it and I feel it."

Aside from confirming Gumbrecht's claim about presence, Toussaint also authenticates the potential violence of fandom when he sketches his own participation in the bad behavior of soccer fanatics in his book *Football*, which includes "Zidane's Melancholy" as an appendix. Toussaint writes in another text that "football allows you to be, not nationalistic, which would have a detestable political connotation that leaves me entirely cold, and not even patriotic, but *chauvinistic*, by which I mean a non-duped, second-level nationalism, an *ironic nationalism*" that grants "a simple-minded comfort, the more flavorsome for being accompanied by a temporarily acceptable intellectual regression. I become biased, aggressive, vehement, combative, I insult the referee, I curse and castigate him. I vilify the other team. I give free rein to the impulses of violence and aggression that normally have no place in my personality. I agree to stupidity and ordinariness. I award myself a treat—let's call it catharsis."

This slightly alarming self-portrait by a "mild-mannered" intellectual brings us to the heart of the matter. It shows no one should pretend that only the poor, uneducated, drunk, and bloodthirsty act repugnantly in the stadium or in front of their screens. The potential for violence will always be present so long as we don't reconfigure fundamental positions that go deeper than noetic convictions. Toussaint's confession of game-time aggression and my family's bigoted interjections sketch the problem of spectatorship, whose bloated, warped shadow envelops everything when we perceive action to be at a distance. By relishing in temporary regressions while giving in to passively viewing, we make ourselves vulnerable to what philosopher Hannah Arendt called the banality of evil. In certain circumstances, we may even act reprehensibly when the responsibility for our actions can be placed on others or when there are no obvious consequences, like on Reddit or Twitter.

Not willing to see the situation as being totally hopeless, Arendt offers an antidote in her writings. Her answer is thought, thinking. Thinking for Arendt is "an ever-present faculty in everybody" that drives us beyond what we already know. It compels us to pose questions whose answers are, in a way, unknowable. Murky as these issues may be, they demand that we create meaning. But, Arendt intones, thinking does not yield foolproof results—once you've thought of something, you cannot check it off the to-do list forever. Meaning has to be made, again and again. And, Arendt says, this quest should nudge us to action. Or, as the German poet and thinker Johann Wolfgang von Goethe said: "Moreover, I hate everything which merely instructs me without increasing or directly quickening my activity."

Characterized by plurality ("the condition of human action because we are all the same, that is, human, in such a way that nobody is ever the same as anyone else who ever lived, lives, or will live") and freedom (the capacity to make new beginnings), action for Arendt requires us to actively make ourselves present to each other through what we say and do. As such, meaning is not antithetical to presence. We just need to come together and begin anew to think together. And I would like to. Take two. Action.

Cue: "I award myself a treat—let's call it catharsis."

Greek for cleansing, purgation or purification, catharsis is a critical notion for understanding spectatorship and one that has been debated since the Ancient Greeks philosophized in the steamy gymnasium. It was Aristotle who first used catharsis to describe what happens to the public, the spectators, when they witness a Tragedy. Roughly, Aristotle's idea is this: after some hours watching a Tragedy whose portrayed events arouse feelings of "pity and fear," you're supposed to expel negative emotions (in tears) and leave the theater feeling refreshed and renewed. In this view, the poet's words are like charcoal filters: when you pass through them, you emerge as pure as crystal clear water.

It is a strategy that has been implemented for centuries and can be felt whenever you say, "Don't go in there!" to a character in a horror film. By exhibiting pity for a hero or heroine who has less awareness of the situation than you do in the safety of your movie seat, you are said to flush out any excess emotion in your system and so restore your natural balance. This idea, however, has not been without critics. Even before Aristotle, Plato criticized our relationship to poetry and theatrical spectatorship. Plato believed mimesis (the imitation of events, which happens in traditional plays) only brings the writer and recipient further from the Truth. As such, Plato concluded, those who dabble in it—poets—should be expatriated from his famed Republic. If poets were allowed to stay and practice their trade, they would only bring us further from the Truth and fan the flames of passion, a bad habit that causes suffering.

Plato's verdict is definitely troublesome if we put all our faith in reason. Yet, if we follow Gumbrecht (as well as William James) and believe knowledge is not purely conceptual, then we have to concede the emotions we feel while reading a poem or watching a TV series are not irrelevant. And besides, who says poets don't tell the truth? Or that fiction isn't its own kind of truth? In my experience, a good poem asks me to think and feel with its string of syllables, images, propositional content, and music; and a great poem demonstrates that its totality is not arbitrary. It leads me to make meaning from all of its elements. In a way, Plato is right. A poem is not the truth—it is an indication. Or, borrowing a metaphor from the Zen tradition, a poem is not the moon, it is a finger pointing at the moon.

Take, for example, Rainer Maria Rilke's "Archaic Torso of Apollo," which we've already considered:

We never knew his head and all the light
that ripened in his fabled eyes. But
his torso still burns like a streetlight dimmed
in which his gaze, lit long ago,

holds fast and shines. Otherwise the surge
of the breast could not blind you, nor a smile
run through the slight twist of the loins
toward that center where procreation flared.

Otherwise this stone would stand cut off
and cold under the shoulder's transparent drop
and not glisten like a wild beast's fur;

and not break forth from all its contours

like a star: for there is no place
that does not see you. You must change your life.

—translated by Edward Snow

This poem, which contemplates the muscularity and physical presence of an Ancient Greek statue, has a startling final line that always leaves me bowled over. In this poem about spectating a figure whose head is missing, I am implicated into an experience and put in relation to the torso as well as the person who is looking at it. While I look over Rilke's shoulder, both of us are drawn to an invigorating conclusion.

You must change your life.

This poem challenges me. But it also reminds me that even if the world is broken, it still possesses beauty and power, and that everything is interconnected. Rilke expresses this in the semantics and diction as well as through the poem's movement. Grappling with an experience, Rilke also couches the complexity in negation before the final revelation, a revelation that extends beyond the particulars. A poem like this does not offer cathartic purgation. The poem is not cleansing. It throws me the mop and tells me to get busy. Or: as a finger pointing at the moon, the poem asks me to bear witness to reality and act responsibly. In the poem's tenderness, there is some relief, but it is the relief of a hot towel doled out after some turbulence just as the captain announces the onset of more turbulence.

While the world of high culture has cut back on the hot towels during its intercontinental hauls and has purposefully steered into the turbulence since modernism, writers and thinkers like

Toussaint and Gumbrecht still need a fix of catharsis, which is why they turn to sports. In the passages quoted above, Toussaint seems to believe we can expunge our inner agitation and realign our inner constitutions after screaming at the screen. The problem of associating sports with cathartic purgation, however, is that it doesn't explain the dramatic spike of domestic violence directly after major sporting events. It also ignores the fact that, for Aristotle, catharsis is directly linked to anagnorisis, the moment when characters come to terms with their own responsibility. That is, the release in a Greek Tragedy only happens after a reconciliation with reality. As such, catharsis might be better associated with reestablishing a connection with the world.

Should we interpret catharsis like this, we can see why sports are empowering and not purifying. They equip us with tools to deal with the world. Youth coaches, young athletes, and non-helicopter parents will agree: sports provide an opportunity to be better in tune with who you are and who you want to be. If you can incorporate your game-time impressions of plurality and freedom into your everyday life, then a new sense of power can be experienced. You can figure out how to react to stress calmly and in control. You can act and not be overwhelmed with worries about the past, and you can do it together. This is an indirect way of saying power comes from unifying presence and meaning.

Arendt again: "Power is actualized only where word and deed have not parted company, where words are not empty and deeds not brutal, where words are not used to veil intentions but to disclose realities, and deeds are not used to violate and destroy but to establish relations and create new realities." Power for Arendt is the capacity to act "in concert" for public and political purposes. But in order for everyone, even those on the sidelines, to act in concert, it is necessary to rethink the role of spectators. This is an old problem and one that Bertolt Brecht grappled with almost a hundred years ago.

Unhappy with the famous fourth wall separating the stage from the spectators, the action from the living, Brecht wanted theatergoers to stop merely consuming theatrical experiences. A fan of boxing, Brecht first tried to solve this riddle by making it known that spectators should talk loudly and smoke cigars during performances like they did at matches. Acting in this manner would change the theatergoers' viewing habits as well as help them stay awake from the hit of nicotine after a solid pre-performance meal. You might then think glazed-over food-coma eyes were what led Brecht to reexamine theater's potential. In fact, it was his political convictions and the emerging discourse in the avant-garde theaters of Berlin in the 1920s.

Utilizing the previously developed techniques of interruption—like pressing pause and freezing the frame in a film—as well as an expansion on Japanese Noh theater's estrangement effect—which would hinder the viewers from identifying with the characters on stage, since the actors themselves did not identify with the characters—Brecht developed his "epic theater" as an attack on mimesis and catharsis as well as on the kinds of theater they produce. "What liberation is this," he wondered, "given that at the end of all these plays, which worked happily only because of the spirit of their time (providence—the moral order), we live a dream-like execution that punishes exaltations as much as debaucheries?" Brecht's early- to mid-career plays all toy with our expectations and are purposefully anticlimactic.

They evade the seemingly logical nature of a play's culmination. By leaving the conclusions of his plays open, Brecht believed the spectators would not succumb to the entrenched expectation of cathartic purgation and would, instead, feel called to political action. Unable to find a resolution in the comfort of a theater seat, they would bring it into being in the world.

Brecht made a number of attempts to rebuke catharsis and mimesis to achieve this purpose, yet eventually abandoned his full-frontal attack in his late plays. "We who are concerned to change human as well as ordinary nature," Brecht writes in 1951, "must find means of 'shedding light on' the human being." At this stage of his career, Brecht ditched his earlier proclivity for irritants. He now felt that such an examination had to be "both beautiful and entertaining."

During his most radical phase, however, Brecht explored "learning-plays" and sketched notes for a learning-play theory in the early 1930s. Like his other early work, these abrasive plays were supposed to dialectically teach people the correct way to live—if only by accurately formulating the problem and showing the failures of wrong answers. These highly didactic and polemic pieces differ from his later work in that the learning-plays were developed for the participants and not the audience, who, in the theory's most radical formulations, wouldn't even be invited to the presentation. Like Montessori schools, Brecht believed here in "learning by doing": "the learning-play teaches by being played and not by being seen. No spectator is necessary for the learning-play, nevertheless he can be utilized." When Brecht wrote these plays, he intended them to be performed by amateur actors and not by professionals. They were made, in a way, for active spectators.

Brecht tested ways to get the public involved, but he still had to sell tickets. Setting aside his revolutionary aims and political convictions for a second, we might remember Brecht was running a theater and had a family to feed—as well as collaborators and mistresses (whom he "worked with" and "borrowed from"). Brecht was a cigar-smoking businessman who loved women and a good fight, and when he realized the audience was not willing to jump into the ring in Berlin's theater scene in the early 1930s, he tried to get the public more involved by handing out surveys after the play and inviting audience members to come back and discuss what they had seen at a later date. As you might imagine, this effort was essentially imperfect. But it was a start. And it was my start as well.

When I moved to Berlin in August 2005—with the official reason to study Brecht's learning-play theory and its influence on his successor Heiner Müller—I concentrated on the more radical formulations of the theory, the role the learning-plays played in Brecht's court appearance at the House of Un-American Activities Committee, and how Müller navigated staging Brecht and his own learning-play *Mauser* outside of East Germany. While this theory and its iterations were invigorating, I began to panic as I immersed myself in the material. I couldn't reconcile becoming a scholar of a theory and praxis that demanded no outsiders with the disinterested distance academic work requires. I tried to explain to myself that a scholar was Brecht's "utilized spectator," although my time in the archives felt like the opposite. I was not the referee or the Greek chorus interacting with the players, I was the Blog Boy blathering in the nosebleeds about what he thinks should happen while his friend pukes in the hood of the sweatshirted gentleman in front of him. I was frustrated. With myself and my struggle to make Brecht's idea of active spectatorship breathe again. If I agreed with Heiner Müller that "utopian moments" are only achieved by breaking through boundaries, what good was I doing standing on the sidelines, judging everything that was already history? Although I no longer discredit the work of academics and am now deeply indebted to the work of Melanie, who has taught me so much about different ways of looking at the Western tradition, this period of estrangement showed me what I was really after: I wanted in on the action.

So, just as I had done in my driveway on Warr Road, I practiced and copied my idols. Writing on reams of staff paper (since I considered these first efforts to be etudes, or studies), I worked on a learning-play, distilling its lessons, translating them to today. With what I hoped would be the literary equivalent of Dream Shakes, skyhooks, and double-clutch layups, as well as something totally unprecedented, *Dogs, Wolves, Coyotes*, my first and only play, was staged for a single night at the English Theater Berlin in 2007. It was an overambitious piece, but I am thankful for the opportunity that came out of it. My learning-play set the stage for an even bigger failure when I was asked to take part in a performance party at the theater later in the summer.

My plan for the evening was very simple. I would bring photocopies of Müller's learning-play *Mauser* in German and English and read it in the theater's foyer. If someone stopped to spectate, I would hand them a copy in whatever language they preferred, show them where I was, and ask them to read with me. The play only has one character, a bit part, and a chorus, so I figured I only needed to find one other person. Together, we would already be an ensemble.

I secured my main actor in a drunken Scotsman after only a couple of minutes. As he sloshed his way through the first page, I was pleased to see the ball rolling. It wasn't long before a number of people from a number of nations gathered. A chorus assembled in two languages and multiple accents. All sticky and glistening from the summer evening, we were loud and in concert and flying high and playing with our voices. Then, I stopped everything. Using the Brechtian interruption, I asked everyone what they thought was happening and why. What did the play mean to them? Could they identify with the situation? Was there a story anyone would like to share? Before the discussion could really get going, the organizers shut down my performance. It was too loud, too rambunctious, too—I refuse to believe or repeat it. For it would imply what I am most afraid of. That this kind of interaction is not desired, not even among creative people.

I am ashamed to admit that at the first sign of adversity I quit. I wasn't strong enough to follow in the footsteps of my idols. Afterward, when I was divorced and still "partially disabled," I became a spectator to life, which at the time seemed to be happening out there, away from me, distant. I took no responsibility for myself or others.

But there is no reason to go back to that beginning again.

There's no need for self-flagellation.

Or even a perfect unified theory.

As Donna Haraway writes, "We do not need a totality to work well."

We only need to want to unite words with deeds, and I want to.

So, let me start over.

But first, let me put some respect on Brecht's name, with one of his poems:

"Oh Joy of Beginning"

Oh joy of beginning! Oh early morning!
The first grass after it's been forgotten
What green is. Oh first page of the book
You were looking forward to, so unexpected. Read
Slowly, very soon
What's unread will be too thin for you. And the first
Splash of water on your sweaty face! A fresh
Cool shirt! Oh beginning of love! Glance that strays!
Oh beginning of work! Pouring oil
Into the cold machine! The first pull and the first hum
Of the starting engine! And the first drag
Of smoke filling your lungs! And you
New thought!

                            —Translated by Shane Anderson

Competition

ON FINDING A HOME AND LEARNING FROM OTHERS
September 25, 2018

Today is the twenty-fifth of September and I am standing in the living room with my pants around my ankles. I am holding a plastic container of mint green jelly, whose demulcent contents I am reluctant to rub into my right thigh and knee because the menthol and camphor will lower my skin temperature even more on this first, real day of autumn in our new apartment, where the boiler lurches and clatters whenever I mash the thermostat's unfamiliar buttons, a reaction that makes me afraid of losing what I wanted for so long. The plumber's receptionist understood me. On the phone this morning, she recommended not succumbing to the *nicht ungefährliches* kettling even though the boiler's violence could escalate before one of their employees could come sometime toward the end of next week—after all, the entire, long summer was erased in one evening and it was so cold this morning she cursed not having gloves on her bike ride to work. I agreed. The raw morning air that had inspired intensified prayers from the starlings in our courtyard before dawn certainly appealed to satisfying basic needs. But instead of relying on the disgruntled boiler processing the city's hard water, I have chosen this tub of horse balm as my blanket, to embrace its contradiction in my body. So, sitting now at our dining table, rubbing this semi-soft substance that smells of menthol and maybe eucalyptus into my leg, I am waiting in this room of fifteen degrees Celsius in the apartment we moved into in August for the arnica and menthol and camphor and rosemary to stimulate my circulation, for it to heat up the slathered muscles from within. Cold to the touch and colder the more it is rubbed in, my skin pricks up with the new information and the crowns of the trees quiver on the other side of the window, they swing, as I suck wind through my teeth. On the German first floor of the north- and west-facing wing of the building, Melanie and I live just under the courtyard's canopy, the enchanted density that has recently been a battleground between the French costume designer living in the front building and the Turkish facility manager, Herr Cat, who asked me to call him Osman. Osman keeps clearing away the piles of freshly fallen walnut and oak leaves that will rot and stink once winter thaws into spring because it is his job to keep the building tidy. Osman would have liked for me to approve of his rigor when he removed three windows with cracked panes in our apartment yesterday, but I couldn't help nudging him in the other direction: I think Catherine wants to grow roses, I said. Osman, full of wisdom, nodded. Sand is what a pearl needs to sparkle and in time the humus will be the rose's allurement and protection, its future contradiction. Which, I guess, is also why I have this nearly luminescent goop matting my leg hairs, sticking them together. This form of topical penance is fertilizer, a translation. Of my quads that screamed like a child greeting the world after I played two hours of full court basketball last night with an intensity I have not reached since developing tendonitis in both of my knees at the age of eleven. I had been unlucky enough to be born into a body that was not forged to become an athlete, the only thing I wanted at the time. I had bad knees, a bad back, and my vision was in need of correction. Still, I hid my history with a failed body from all the coaches I solicited in emails yesterday morning, where I asked whether their team was searching for new players with experience going back decades. Of the four clubs that replied almost immediately, I was most excited by DBC Berlin, a team that was holding practice the same day around the corner. I liked that they were close, and I liked that their 1. *Vorsitzender*, Tom, decorously replied to my follow-up question about getting into the gym with the words, "through the door." It suggested that this team might be playing with the kind of attitude I wanted. Not testosterone-driven competition with loads of yelling and accusations, but with fun and humor. By choosing the team closest to me, however, I realized how much further I needed to go to achieve my vaguely defined goals. The nervousness and confusion that plagued me as I pushed against a number of locked doors on the outside of the building did not dissipate when I had the ball in my hands and my defender put pressure on me. Holding my breath, I tried to get the ball anywhere else as quickly as possible, which, in the first two games to 11, was by launching a forced shot with my body out of position, out of rhythm, a rhythm I had been working to establish for more than four years. Having tweaked my foot placement by observing my foot imprints on the snow on the court near Melanie's old apartment in winter and watching my arms' shadows in the summer after I launched the ball into the air on Tempelhofer Feld, my continual desire had been to create a single fluid motion with a considerable extension of my arms, and I had spent countless hours getting a sunburn or cold chasing the ball, brick after brick, then swish after swish, learning the importance of proper mechanics. Then my form drastically improved last year when I watched a video of Klay Thompson where he demonstrated how a player could shoot with greater consistency—like him—describing his shot as a "reverse waterfall," a fluid motion from the toes all the way up to the fingers. I did my best to imitate this and not shoot like Draymond Green, who looks like he's wearing a backpack full of bricks. The first lesson I took from all those hours outdoors after watching the short video was to establish a position, balance, even in a shaky situation. Which was what I found difficult to put into practice in the well-lit gym that had a laminated floor with all these players who were much better than I expected. I kicked my feet forward and moved my upper body away from the basket every time I launched the ball from my chest, a position that is too low for a shot to not get blocked. I jumped so quickly that I forgot all about bending my knees, my rhythm. I was already anticipating a problem, a blocked shot or unwanted contact from my opponent, which meant I had allowed the defense to determine what I was doing from the beginning. Part of this had to do with my back. I hadn't informed any of the team members, who came from all over the world, about my surgery or my inhibited bending ability from the rods' inflexibility. I sometimes forget my limitations and I was too proud to notify them once I noticed I couldn't get low on defense. My lack of execution would then be asterisked at best as the failing effort of someone who was physically incapable—something I refuse to believe.

Frustrated and drenched in sweat between the third and fourth game, I caught the attention of one team member, Sami, who gave me some tips. He had watched the way I played, and he told me to stand up straight to knock down the shots he had seen me make during warm-ups. All I needed, he said, was to remain calm and trust in my abilities. I thanked him and tried to not get too emotional. For he had given me a gift by finding the words I was not yet able to express: I had come here to find my trust in difficult situations and not give in to anxiety. To do the right thing, for myself, my team, my ecology, without ever letting myself get too comfortable or lazy or scared or self-loathing. Months later, after another teammate, Ferhat, commented upon my continual improvement in the locker room with all the others, I was shocked to discover that this was what it actually took to be good. Trust. Faith that you can do it. Although this wouldn't begin to congeal until later, right now it is, admittedly, becoming unbearable. My left leg is freezing in comparison to my right one, covered in the horse balm. Taking out another handful of the ooze to create a balance between my legs, this further application creates a time delay, an echo in my skin, a reverberation between my lower limbs. I somewhat grumpily pull up my jogging pants and stand up. I remember what it felt like years ago to rub Vicks Vaporub on my genitals and I smile. I can feel all of my butt muscles, which is not entirely disagreeable. I consider walking down our very long corridor (our corridor!) to wash my hands in the bathroom then decide against it. I'll probably put some more on my sore shoulder later. I wipe my hands on my jogging pants then sit down again. I hit the spacebar and return to what I was doing before. There's a close-up of Klay Thompson on the screen and he is shrugging off his second foul in the first minute of Game 7 of the 2018 Western Conference finals against the Houston Rockets. I know it won't be long before he is called for a third foul and will be forced to sit out for the rest of the first half, which the Rockets will dominate. When I first saw this game live in the middle of the night in May, it had taken all of my willpower to not go out and buy a pack of cigarettes at the 24-hour kiosk around the corner from Melanie's old apartment. The season was about to end because of fouls, and the atmosphere was very hostile in the Rockets' arena. I could literally feel the anxiety that the pressure was squeezing out of all the players. With a bit of distance, I am now studying this game, which the Warriors won on their way to their third championship in four years, to see, play by play, how the Warriors eased into themselves and took the game over. I want to see whether there are any perceivable moments when the Warriors overcame their difficulties and I want to know what happened before them. More than this, I want to watch every play to learn any fundamental knowledge that I can apply next week at practice, which is actually just a bunch of guys playing pick-up, hence the need to find coaching elsewhere. With the Rockets' two free throws already over, the Warriors bring the ball up the court. Kevin Durant has his back to the basket and is establishing position around the elbow on the right side of the court. When Draymond Green passes him the ball, Durant's defender tips the entry pass away and creates a turnover. I rewind the play and press pause. I search "establishing post position" in another tab full of basketball wisdom and read what it has to say. I then hit the spacebar again and see what I have already seen. I think as I watch the play again that maybe Durant didn't whip his leg quickly or strongly enough and I wonder whether this was why Green was yelling at him after the play transpired. I hit the spacebar again to pause the game and write "get low and wide in the seal then keep the ball at my chin with my arms extended" with a mechanical pencil that is sticking to my sticky fingers. These words come after "run wide in transition and keep looking over my shoulder" on the sheet of paper with the logo of my father's defunct business as a heading, words I had written while watching Kevon Looney continually look at Stephen Curry on the Warriors' previous play that also frustratingly resulted in a turnover. With these two notes only a minute and thirty seconds into the most nerve-wracking game of last season, I have already answered two of my biggest questions about last night. I had often been lost in transition and got overpowered in the post. After a rebound from one or another of my teammates, I had run full speed into the corner and missed three passes from Călin, who had seen that I had a clear path to the basket. I had also shuffled my feet on the lower block and travelled, since I didn't have a strong stance that could take the bump from Georg's larger frame, which I feared might accidentally hit the rods or on one of the screws that goes deep into my body. Last night, this fear was not apparent for more than an instant. The only thing that was apparent was that I was a failure. Melanie laughed when I came home and said such. She tried to console me. It was a difficult situation. It was like a blind date with nine other men in very little clothes. *They are all familiar with one another and you're new to all of them. Let it go.* She was right. I was playing to be liked and that was ugly. I was so worried about doing the right thing that I often couldn't do the right thing. Luckily, I made my second basket, a game-winning three, in the final match.

This, I was sure, was what secured my invitation for next week and what opened up some garrulity in the locker room afterward. I had readied myself for the guarded interactions I am familiar with in new contexts in Germany, but Viktor even asked me about my occupation, which I answered, atypically, with the truth. When this senior member of the team, a curly-haired hippie in his early 50s, asked me what I was writing about, my answer was "you" with my eyes before I shifted to a combination of fact and fiction. I wasn't there to speak about being a writer or writing, which often sounds more exciting to outsiders. The inner life of a writer is as exceptional as everyone else's—it's only that the writer cultivates it like flowers to be sold on the market. To give yourself is the greatest gift and that's why I admire athletes as well as everyone else who is willing to do this whole-heartedly in whatever they do. But I didn't say this. I just thanked them for having me, then left. I was tired from running up and down the court for so long. And I am tired now, pleasantly so. My legs are both agreeable, warm, and as I hit the spacebar again, the game's intensity increases with each possession. Fouls are committed, the ball is turned over, shots are being missed. Without hitting pause, I write down "mistakes happen—~~get over it~~ recover from them." Become the pearl the oyster makes from the grain of sand, let go of the play before. Hit the delete button. There is no smooth mountain to climb, and if you slip, stand up, it happens. I climb back into the game, not taking notes now, just watching the drama unfold. I keep watching the frantic game play until Thompson commits his third foul on a closeout with eight minutes left to play in the first quarter. Even now, it is an emotional game and I can barely stand watching despite knowing the outcome. I am happy though that I no longer have the desire to smoke. One of the broadcast's commentators, Chris Webber—my childhood favorite player, an ex-Warrior, who is now an announcer for TNT—talks about the aggressiveness of the Rockets. Both teams needed to come out ready to compete, Webber says, and the Rockets are doing it. It feels stupid to ask but I don't know what he actually means. Aren't all of these professional athletes coming out to compete? Surely no one wants this to be the final game of the season! Although this might have just been broadcaster speak to fill time with voices, it does occur to me that competition is taken for granted. In that podcast with the Positive Coaching Alliance, all Kerr had said about his fourth core value was that competition was obvious, that "it almost goes without saying." This may be true in sports, where it is seen as something positive, but competition is always shaded as fighting against something, an opponent, and it is usually perceived as being negative in the circles I am in. It suggests that someone is self-interested and not nurturing their ecology. Moreover, competition has a note of violence and this is in our language. Even in the world of competitive sports. We say the Warriors *beat* the Rockets. The Rockets were *smacked, hammered, destroyed* in the second half of the third quarter, etc. And just look at the team names: Warriors, Rockets, Cavaliers, Raptors, Trail Blazers, etc. The world is framed as competing interests, fears molded into conventions, hatred that is taken for granted. If this is what Kerr means, it seems difficult to align this with his other core values, especially when they are applied off the court, as was his intention. There is a way, I think, to see what Kerr means that is not predicated on violence. If you shift your focus away from the victors and listen to the postgame press conferences of the losing team, competition becomes more intricate. The team will say, "We got beat," just as often as "We didn't compete," or "We didn't execute according to our game plan," or "We weren't playing our game" (that is, if they don't blame everything on the refs). In fact, the same goes for the victors. Players will commend their coaches for coming up with a good game plan, as well as one another for executing, and it is bad form to report on the failures of your opponents. When Kevin Durant gave his press conference after winning his first championship in 2017, he kept deferring to the other players on the Warriors when the reporters tried to make everything about him, the Finals MVP. "What about Patrick McCaw?" he challenged. "What about Zaza Pachulia to start the game?" What about Steph Curry, coming in like a "big dog," and what about Andre Iguodala with twenty points off the bench? It was a collective effort, they worked toward their goal together. Competition, then, doesn't need to be seen as negative. Competition could be seen as striving toward your goals and overcoming the obstacles the opponent presents. To approach the game like this activates the other core values. Doing such is not causal—you do not go down the list one after the other. Rather, as I'm learning, acting according to the Warriors' four core values is a system of entanglement. Each value feeds into the other and is interdependent on them. It's a celebration—and right now I was slowly getting it: you need to be practicing the other core values in order for competition to really click. That is, if you play with joy and focus and compassion for others, the things you are competing for will be more important than any language related to destruction. There is in fact very little you can do if you act out of fear or negligence or self-serving interests that will not eventually end in fear or negligence or self-serving interests. The only counter is to not engage with it, to go beyond it. You don't plough through your opponent—you step around them. In basketball, it's called a Euro step. And right now, I'd like to step around this difficult sequence. I want to see how the Warriors stop beating themselves with turnovers and bad fouls. I want to shift my focus. I click on the third quarter in the window for NBA League Pass, which I have subscribed to for almost three seasons now. When I click, the video freezes. I am watching this game from the internet connection we are temporarily borrowing from our upstairs neighbors and it is not always reliable. Unlike them, our friends, Julia and Bakri, who helped us find this apartment. They had kept us on the job for eight months after our rejected initial attempt to become *Nachmieter* of the former tenants. In that time, we learned that the apartment was going to be renovated, which meant that our dream flat, the one where we'd have part of our community closer to home, was destined to be too expensive. We gave up on the idea of moving out of Melanie's small flat and focused on being grateful for what we had. It wasn't nice to have to slide out of bed in the bedroom that was literally that, a room for a bed, to go to the toilet at night but we could be thankful that we had a bed and a toilet of our own, unlike my mother. Then, a day came in June 2018 when I had to renew my work visa at the eternally terrifying foreigners office, a place where all immigrants without oodles of cash are treated like parasites and whose staff once explained to me that the toilets in the men's room didn't have seats and were just holes with molding for your feet because most immigrants didn't know how to use them, "they only know how to shit in a hole in the ground" (it was unclear if he meant me or someone else since he was using the word *Sie*, which in spoken language sounds exactly the same, it can either be the formal "you" or the plural third person). That June morning, I was diligently putting my paperwork together in those plastic transparencies German bureaucrats love, because it shows that you are serious and *ordentlich*, when the phone rang. Would we be interested in seeing the place now that they were finished with the renovations? I was curious just to see what they had done, even if it was too expensive. We could be there at 4 PM after my visa appointment. *Abgemacht*. Melanie was surprised. We had agreed to be happy with what we had, each other. And we had grown tired of all the small comments of surprise at me being the one who was the foreigner and that we spoke English together, even though we were both fully capable of speaking only in German. Whenever we got this comment, the gatekeepers—I mean real estate agents—had assumed that Melanie, who is half Indian, was the foreigner until they saw a copy of her German passport. Never sure if this was racist, we just acted like the rental agencies were looking for some kind of security we were unable to offer—perhaps because my visa was expiring. We may have been lucky that I had just received a new visa when we arrived at the beautifully refurbished apartment around the corner from Winterfeldtplatz but we were very surprised that the old lady acting as the "extended arm" of the owner didn't know what an apartment like this could go for today. In all of our research and experience, we knew they could have asked almost double. We tried to suppress it but felt lucky when the woman said we could have the apartment and we high-fived when we got home. There it is again. Luck. Luck, luck, luck, luck, luck. But then maybe our getting this place had nothing to do with luck. Maybe we fit into the owners' scheme of tenants. Like our friends and the other neighbors I have met, we are from here and not, and we artists and thinkers living in the *Land der Dichter und Denker*. Or maybe, and this is what I now believe, we previously had the wrong idea of competition. Melanie and I had been fighting for a little more than two years against having separate apartments or not enough space in one of them, and not for what we really wanted, which was to be together, always. I'll never know for certain why we got the apartment, but the video is still buffering and I'm getting impatient. I click on another tab I have opened. The Warriors' official channel. It is an exciting time of the year: training camp has started, and the basketball season is about to begin. Yesterday was the last media day the Warriors will ever hold in Oakland and I am feeling a little nostalgic. This will be the last season the Warriors play in Oracle Arena, the place where I attended my first professional basketball game. Back then, RUN TMC was in full effect and the high scorer of that night was Šarūnas Marčiulionis, the Lithuanian Hall of Fame player who was responsible for bringing the Euro step to America. I remembered that Marčiulionis is also someone I had the honor to speak to when I was in Lithuania in 2017 to present some of the research for this book at the Contemporary Art Center's Reading Room in Vilnius, and who told me over the phone that he wore the number 13 because he had often been the thirteenth man on the Soviet teams in the early 1980s and was thus cut from the international competitions. When he came to America to play for the Warriors and Don Nelson, he wanted to remember the importance of perseverance and he contained this in his number. *Perseverance*, I wrote that down. It's like Gumbrecht says: what we want most in life is the hardest to obtain. And then I reflected that perseverance will also be important for the current Warriors team in 2018–19, who seemed fatigued toward the end of last season. Next year, in 2019, the Warriors will be moving to the Chase Center in San Francisco and there is a bittersweet note to Kerr's press conference. There will be a lot of difficult financial decisions the team will have to make and he reminds us that all good things come to an end. The Warriors will be leaving Oakland, which had been home to the Warriors for 47 years. We should enjoy this version of this team and Oracle Arena while we can. When this short video is over, I open another page I have tabulated since the video of the game still refuses to load. It is a conversation with David West, who just played with the Warriors for the final two seasons of his career, winning back-to-back championships in 2016–2017 and 2017–2018. West is convinced this will be the Warriors' toughest year yet. Every team has had years to adjust to the ways the Warriors play, and the Warriors will have to make adjustments themselves. West emphasizes that contrary to what everyone thinks, the Warriors faced a number of problems that they had to overcome together the previous season. They had to continually compete for their goals; their winning wasn't destined. I read a little further into the interview and West is now talking about social issues. He says, "We've got to sort of change our orientation as a society. I'm always focused on peace and justice. Everybody's on the Colin Kaepernick train, but nobody understands what the message is. Kap's message is a message of peace, is a message of justice. We want a system that's just for all people, and we want people to be governed in their realities, their social orientation to be governed by peace. And that's what the world wants." West is referring to the aftermath of Kaepernick's famous act of civil disobedience when he kneeled during "The Star-Spangled Banner" in the fall of 2016. Kaepernick was immediately criticized as being anti-American and for being against the military. Every God-fearing American knows that you stand during the National Anthem to honor those who lost their lives in service for the nation. Kaepernick, however, insisted that he took the knee at the beginning of NFL games to address social injustice and protest the whitewashing of police brutality, the white on Black violence. Kaepernick's kneeling, which resulted in him getting "blackballed" from professional football, sparked his commitment to activism. An activism that has never been an *against*; it is a *for*. It is *for* awareness about injustice that young Black men face every day when they want to do things as simple as walk to the corner store. It is *for* peace and *for* life and *for* liberty, for all.

Suddenly, the children outdoors are making a lot of noise. They have been let out on recess and they are singing and shouting, kicking balls, dribbling them, playing. It's the first month of the term and the pupils at the Catholic school still sound happy to be there, especially to be out on recess. Their courtyard is separated from ours by a half wall a little taller than the ground floor apartment. This allows for their voices to stream their warmth into the courtyard and to wash over the Buddha statue in a niche on our side of the wall. The Buddha doesn't seem to mind. He is quietly meditating and showing the *vitarka mudra*, a gesture that induces the energy of the teacher and teachings as well as discussions of spiritual principles that may also involve arguments. Two of my neighbors, an older German and Japanese couple, also artists, are grateful that the Tibetan Buddhist Center in the front of our house erected this statue for our benefit. This statue is protecting us from the Church, the German artist joked. I had laughed with him, but I had heard that it was mere luck. The monk in the front of the house had said that it was there when he moved in, long before the Dali Lama stayed with him here in this building. Also, I have no reason to distance myself from this particular congregation. In the Second World War, Clemens August Graf von Galen preached that the right "to life, to inviolability, and to freedom is an indispensable part of any moral social order" and openly resisted the Nazis and their racist ideologies. Although best known as the Lion of Münster, von Galen began his ordinance at this congregation just over the wall. To my surprise, the video of the Warriors game starts playing in the background. I can hear a whistle blown. Another Rockets three-pointer has just been missed and a foul was committed on the rebound. When I switch to the page, the video starts buffering again. I click back ten seconds to see what has transpired, and the video hangs. Not even this quick fix is solving my impatience. I can hardly wait for our internet connection to be installed. And I hope this farce isn't disturbing Julia and Bakri. I open the last page I have saved in the browser to wait some more for the stream to buffer. It is the *Guardian* and I scan the headlines. Another woman has accused the 45th president's choice for Supreme Court justice of sexual assault and a man was put in jail in Paris for three months for slapping a woman's behind. Bill Cosby, the father America grew up with in the 1980s, faces prison time for sexual assault. Further evidence has surfaced regarding the Catholic clergy's sexual abuse of children in Germany and I reconsider my alliances. So, too, does the current President of the United States of America. He announces to the United Nations that he will only give money to friends and the UN's environmental program has stopped receiving money from two countries; the head of this department has had questionable spending habits and was a frequent flyer—a contradiction. These are not immediately related. And neither is the end of cleavage being announced. And yet, they are. The only headline where women are subjects is where activist nuns are pressuring Smith & Wesson over gun safety. Amidst all this subtle bigotry, there is one story I consider clicking on. In defiance to the concept of nations, Santiago Sierra has planted the black flag to destroy all borders in Antarctica. I hover over the headline but don't want to jeopardize my bandwidth. Scrolling further, it has been announced that the "left-wing" roughing the passer rule is ruining American football. I can't help but laugh. Safety should not be ideological. The further I scroll into a sports section that begins to concentrate only on soccer I grow tired of looking at the news. It is hard to not give in to fatigue and despair and indifference when the day seems so far away in its endless permutations, and a simple critique of them feels like inspecting the functionality of a smoke detector while the building is still burning. These injustices are my injustices. But how to touch them and let them permeate my skin? There is the problem of over-identification. I have been no stranger to this. As a child, I didn't know that I wasn't Mexican. Or rather, I didn't think it mattered. Sure, I was white but so was Carlos—and he had red hair and freckles. And though I couldn't speak Spanish, I wanted to learn, and my friend Raphy was teaching me a few phrases, mostly things I shouldn't say in front of my mother. For all the years I spent playing basketball with my friends from my neighborhood Bijoux, which used to be the Mexican and Filipino "ghetto" of South Lake Tahoe, it never occurred to me that my skin color represented anything that might be reprehensible to Raphy, Joey, and Freddy until the day they were jumped into the gang Sur 13 at the beginning of seventh/eighth grade. The day after, they had black eyes and cuts and avoided me on the bus. But then Joey approached me once the bus drove around the golf course's meadow and he informed me that he was sorry, their older cousins wouldn't let me join the gang. Sadly, that also meant we could no longer be friends. They could no longer come over to shoot hoops and we could not hang out at the dances at the Rec Center. The problem was I was a *pinche gringo*. Just like Carlos had said. I was devastated. That night, my mom found me in my room crying. I had piled up all of my CDs on my desk, ready to sell them. Tupac and Dr. Dre hated me. It was time to stop living the lie. I was white. I belonged to the same race that beat Rodney King for no reason. I thought I was a good guy. I had always identified with my Mexican and Filipino friends who lived in the apartment complex down the road because we all loved the same thing: basketball. We were hoopers—we knew ball is life. It was also because, although I was definitely incapable of expressing it in these terms, their reality seemed closer to mine than those of the other white children with whom I had gone to elementary school. My parents had misled the school district with a false address—which, lest we forget, is a criminal offense—before my first day of school so that I could attend Sierra House Elementary and not Bijoux Elementary, which was just down the road. My father didn't want me to learn "Mexican" before English and so we drove twenty-five minutes in snowstorms to get to school in the morning. There, my best friend was the heir apparent to the casino empire on the other side of the state lines, something my father, who had worked at the casino's painting department before opening his own business, was infinitely proud of. I was class hopping even before I knew what that meant! For Kris Ledbetter's eleventh birthday, I was invited to join his family at the most expensive joint in town, a restaurant on the top floor of his family's hotel/casino with a magnificent view of the lake. I was nervous. Would Kris' parents be upset that I showed up in a polo shirt and not the suit they had requested in the invitation? There was nothing we could do about that. I didn't own a suit. What we could do is figure out what I should order. My father told me to go for the lobster. If they're paying, of course. He gave me thirty dollars just in case they were cheapskates and when Kris' father gave me the go-ahead, it was on him, I requested lobster. It was impossible. They were out. Now I had to choose something from the menu whose words were all foreign. The waiter recommended the scampi with linguine. Both were new to me, but I agreed without hesitation. When the food arrived, I was relieved to find shrimp and pasta on my plate, even though it was in some unidentifiable sauce. I was a little disappointed. They didn't have cocktail sauce for the shrimp like they did at Sizzler. I asked for the sauce and everyone laughed. I was too embarrassed to use the bottle the waiter brought for me. I refresh the video completely to escape this memory. It still won't load. That's OK. I have learned enough fundamentals for the day. Be stable, aware of the action at all times, and establish a position. Take what comes to you, don't force the issue, and don't defer out of convenience. If the play is there, take it. Follow through. Be vulnerable, uncomfortable, never defend yourself. Build relationships. Test your limits, extend them. Make reparations. By being better on the next play and breaking your habits. Keep working toward your goal of living in joy, mindfulness, and compassion; and compete for it. Stay with it. You cannot do this for anyone except yourself. But you can build alliances, kinships, whose interests won't ever be identical. Accept that they are not you and admit that you are not better than them. Extend a helping hand if it is needed. If someone doesn't want your help, like my mother doesn't, respect their decisions. Wait. Melanie just texted and now it is late November. She's on her way home from work and we have a date. *Today is a good day*, reads her next message. A euphemism for her fertility. Thankfully I have quit smoking, minus the small hiccup after the Camp Fire in Paradise, something that had always made me worried when we talked about having a child. I respond with some lovey-dovey emoticons and stand up to clean up. I ask if she wants anything extra from the organic store, *Speisekammer im Eldorado*, around the corner. When she writes *no* with a thankful emoticon, I am thankful as well. I'm still a little sore from last night's practice, though much less so than before— horse balm is magic!—and I am happy that I don't need to leave the building. Our home. I take a deep breath. I look in the mirror that's still leaning against the wall. I flex. Not bad. I smile at myself. But I also look a little worried. I am scared of becoming a father, of not being good enough. I laugh. Haven't I learned anything? I turn on the heater. What could go wrong?

A New Hope

ON THE END OF AN ERA,

OFF THE RECORD WITH ANDRE IGUODALA

March 18, 2020—April 15, 2020

March 18 in Germany: 12,327 positive; 2,960 new cases; 31 new recoveries; 2 new deaths. The mask I bought for myself was black like the plague, like death, it suggests that no one escapes—not Laszlo the grocer or Thanos the baker or me, who just purchased these black or yellow-and-blue masks for my family from Olga the tailor so that we can protect one another when Melanie's parents come to visit their grandson in two weeks at the distance the government deemed safe in these early days of living with the novel corona virus. Although Olga thought the black would look chic on me, I feel like an idiot as I stand in line to get vegetables from Laszlo at the outdoor market. My ears are sticking out of my hat because the mask's elastic bands are too tight, and my glasses are fogging up from my breath's condensation on this otherwise mild early spring morning. I consider taking the mask off as I am the only one on Winterfeldtplatz who is wearing one, then resolve to keep it on for those who put themselves at risk to care for others. There's also the question of illness. If I didn't test positive for

COVID-19 last week, it may have only been because people like me were not being tested yet. Showing symptoms was not sufficient, you also had to have been in contact with someone who tested positive or have been in Italy or China—which may have been true of some of the customers at the bookstore. I had chest pain for three days but then it disappeared, and I was only very, very tired. My doctor told me to not be worried, it didn't have to be COVID. There are other viruses. But I should still stay home for a week. My mask then is a small gesture of solidarity as well as precaution that is currently being interpreted as paranoia from a late middle-aged woman who cuts in front of me at the outdoor market. People are acting hysterical, she tells Laszlo the grocer and by people she means me. I've lived through worse things, she says as she pays for her three limes and two avocados, and I try to imagine what they might be. I almost explain my previous symptoms to her, but I don't want to alarm anyone. My mask is protecting them, which my doctor said after a week without symptoms is enough. I say, I'm just taking things seriously. Unlike the young people who are throwing "corona parties" in the parks and dressing up like superheroes or Adam and Eve. I can't blame them, I would have done the dumb same, and besides everything is very confusing. Some districts in the city are shutting their playgrounds, others are not, restaurants are closed though people can still mill about in front of the restaurant to get takeaway. The woman walks away with her three limes and two avocados. I imagine this will be the last time she cuts in line to only buy ingredients for guacamole. Things are about to change, for everyone, I think. How's the little one? Laszlo asks. He gives me a banana for the boy like always. He's teething, I say, the poor guy's not having the best of times. It's something we all have to go through, Laszlo says, he'll be alright. And he's right. We've all teethed. We'll all get through this. It's just that we're all going to have to change our lives.

March 31 in Germany: 71,808 positive; 4,923 new cases; 2,600 new recoveries; 130 new deaths. Kian is singing into my breastbone as we pass the bags hanging on the fencing on the northside of Winterfeldtplatz. This means he's tired sooner than usual, so I stop in front of the last of the bags intended for the homeless, and zip up my jacket some more for head support. Then I rub Kian's back through the jacket and carrier and tell him to nap. He sings back at me and I smile. I look at the plastic bags that have mostly been ripped open. Of those that are not flapping in the cold wind, most are filled with what looks to be towels and sweat-shirts. There's also one with a can of goulash and a glass of I think pickles. I try to remember whether I saw the goulash and pickles yesterday when Kian and I went for our daily walk. I pinch the mask's wire over my nose, adjust my gloves and shiver. It's cold today and whoever delivered these perishable goods deserves praise. They're not just sorting out their closet out of boredom, they're putting themselves in danger for others by going to the supermarket. It's true what I read on Facebook yesterday. There are more things to admire about people during a pandemic than there are to despise. People are realizing that we're all intercon-nected and we're much more willing to help one another. I remind myself to prepare a bag to bring with me tomorrow and I thank the "you" who gave me the idea to start stocking up on things during that conversation in the bookstore, which Melanie and I have done ever since. Kian sings some more into my chest and we walk past the closed shops on Winterfeldtstraße. "Closed" notices are stuck to all their doors and windows, revealing the various states of desperation, anger, acceptance, and hope of the proprietors. To think that, according to one theory, a farmer ate some diseased meat in a market in central China and now capitalism, climate damage, and our interactions have completely changed. For how long, no one knows. The stay-in-place orders that began on March 23 in Berlin were extended today until after my birthday. Some are saying this could last until there's a vaccine, which could be a year or more. Much of this will depend upon how politicians are responding and I know that we are lucky to be living in Germany. Lucky to have a home, lucky to have one another, lucky, lucky, lucky. I feel a tinge of guilt as I think about my family back in America and wonder whether we'll be free to celebrate our wedding anniversary and Kian's birthday outdoors in August like we planned over Christmas. Then I turn left on Zietenstraße and Kian's head is getting heavy. I hope he can get a good sleep in and that his mother, my wife, Melanie, can work in peace for a while. I brought a book so that I can read in the park if Kian is still sleeping and it doesn't stay so cold that I have to keep moving, which, as I cross Bülowstraße, I am happy to do, it's really very cold. I'm also happy to go on these walks as it helps our ecology now that Melanie's parents can't spend time with their grandson and help us with childcare. Every day since I've been on sick leave, Kian and I have walked to Tiergarten to be among the trees that are almost blooming. Melanie and I have realized that our time is best spent like this as Melanie could be our primary breadwinner and our future would then be more dependent on her having time to work than on me serving customers.

I wait in front of the Twelve Apostles Church at the intersection on Kurfürstenstraße and think that if I did quit the bookstore in the middle of this pandemic then I'd finally have more time for the family and for writing and translating, but as Kian and I walk behind Möbel Hübner, it feels crazy to quit given the likelihood of austerity to deal with colossal debts left by rescue spending. But then, there are "cases where a fact cannot come at all unless a preliminary faith exists in its coming." And Melanie and I believe that I can make it without the bookstore, which I had drifted away from. Kian and I take a left on Kluckstraße. We walk past Magdeburger Platz. People move out of the way of the man with the baby more out of respect than out of fear of the man with the black mask, they smile. I am surprised by how normal this all feels already. Soon masks may even be compulsory. What once felt impossible now feels quotidian. Everything is a question of habits and routines. We have been lucky. Life in lockdown has been easy for us to adjust to. Our radius has been small ever since Melanie entered the late stages of pregnancy and we have gotten used to the idea that our knowledge is tenable. That we are fallible. That life changes fast and you have to adapt to it. I pat Kian on the back for imparting this wisdom as we cross the canal. It starts snowing. I consider waking Kian up to show him his first snow. I don't. He needs his sleep. I keep walking.

April 3 in Germany: 91,159 positive; 6,365 new cases; 2,135 new recoveries; 168 new deaths. Today is different from all the days that preceded it. Those days that remained the same and were filled with waking up, playtime, nap, breakfast, shower, walk, lunch, playtime, nap, cooking, dinner, bedtime, and then writing for me. The rhythm will stay the same but I haven't been a vessel for whatever virus that was for a while, and today we're doing something dangerous, risky. We're going to break the law and meet Melanie's parents in public although assembly of more than two people is forbidden. We can no longer stand it that Kian hasn't seen his grandparents on the other side of the city for a month already. This is why Kian and I are scouring all the park benches in our neighborhood, trying to find two benches apart from one another that are hidden from plain sight but also in what will be the afternoon sun. We've checked all along Winterfeldtplatz, scanned the benches on Maaßenstraße, Nollendorfstraße, and Luitpoldtstraße, and the only ones that meet both requirements are those close to St. Matthias, on the backside, in the church's garden, toward Pallasstraße, which Kian and I are now walking down, having made my decision. Kian is sleeping as we head toward Potsdamerstraße and I consider going to Tiergarten like usual then decide to continue. A cop car passes me on the street, and I wonder whether they would be able to see us if we were sitting in the garden. I feel bad for the police for the first time in my life, they have to put up with our idiocy and won't be protected since the United States allegedly stole face masks from the Berlin police force in an act of modern piracy. I keep walking. I pass under the huge apartment building straddling Pallasstraße from one side of the street to the other, which also hovers above a four-story bunker. Suddenly I realize I have mindlessly been walking to a sacred ground without meaning to. Just on the other side of the bunker is the gym where I play basketball. There it is, three weeks later. It's dark inside and I'm surprised. I miss the physical exercise and the guys and the feelings the game elicits only now that I'm standing here. I wonder how long it will take to get back into shape and become a knockdown shooter with a quick release again. I had surprised myself as I got better at basketball after having invested trust in myself. I tried to stay humble, but I had become silently proud of being able to perform Iguodala's swipe downs. In front of the nondescript gym complex, I stop in my tracks and lament the loss of Iguodala, who was traded after the Warriors lost to the Raptors in the 2019 NBA Finals, then kept walking. This was the only thing Bob Myers could do to salvage some value for the team once Kevin Durant left for the Brooklyn Nets, starting a chain reaction of trades, releases, and retirements. The only players remaining from the 2018–19 Warriors team on the 2019–20 team were Curry, Green, Looney, and Thompson; and Draymond Green was the only one still playing during the 2019–20 season before it was delayed because of COVID-19 and then cancelled for all the teams out of playoff contention, like the Warriors. In any case, the dynasty was over and had been for a while. What was more, the 2018–19 team had lost touch with the four core values. What can you say? It happens? Sometimes you have to press the delete button and start over. Sometimes you have to realize that what you had known doesn't work anymore. And that can be rather dramatic. Someone on Goebenstraße coughs and I snap out of my reveries as I pass another empty storefront then double dip into my thoughts. We were now officially in the After the Oracle era—the Warriors had moved to a new stadium in San Francisco at the beginning of the season. And yet, everything that had been gained had not been entirely lost. The new team of youngsters slowly discovered the four core values during the 2019–20 season. The team wasn't great. In fact, it was famously terrible in terms of record, even for the Warriors of old. It didn't matter. The young players were learning to operate with the Warriors' set of values, as I had, and that can take a while. This is because these values are not a GPS system dictating where to turn and when. They are only a compass with which you can assess whether you're moving in the right direction. To mix metaphors, it takes time to learn a new language and stop translating it back into your mother tongue, and even more time until you can express yourself in the new one without remembering the old. Where am I heading? I'm halfway to U-Bhf Yorckstraße on Goebenstraße and we should be home for lunch in half an hour. I turn around and start walking home. Home. On my way back, I decide to order an indoor hoop to hang on my office door, which is soon to become Kian's bedroom. I guess you could call it indoctrination.

April 15 in Germany: 134,753 positive; 2,543 new cases; 4,400 new recoveries; 309 new deaths. It's hard to believe that we made it to Tiergarten and Kian hadn't started sleeping. We walked past Winterfeldtplatz, the Twelve Apostles Church, Möbel Hübner, the canal, the Federal Ministry of Defense, the German Resistance Memorial and into the park before Kian started crying. I patted his head, which was held in place by the UV protection veil—the sun was shining!—but then he started protesting. He didn't want to sleep, he wanted out. This desire to explore the outdoors was new. I took Kian out of the carrier, an act that is much easier now that it is warm, and started carrying him in my arm. He grew silent. I pointed with my free hand at the magnolia tree, the cherry blossoms, the tulips, the ducks, and the geese. Birds were chirping in the trees and rabbits were playing in the bushes. There was so much to show him, it was incredible. Everything is so new to him, it's hard to not be inspired by his curiosity. We sat down on a bench, took a selfie, and sent it to Melanie. Then I forwarded it to my father, mother and sister, the latter two hadn't met Kian and probably wouldn't until the pandemic is over. We have had much more contact since Kian was born and I actively made a vow to let go of the past. Then I forwarded the selfie to Luciano, who immediately responded with green heart emoticons before telling me that his flight to Berlin was cancelled again. His move to the city was indefinitely delayed. I was sad but what are you going to do? We are living in a pandemic and not everything is possible. Kian yawns. We are still sitting here, listening to the wind in the trees, he's observing who knows what, but it's captivating. On the field in front of us, there are children throwing frisbees, kicking balls, and flying kites. People are reading on blankets, doing Tai Chi or leg stretches, and talking to friends. Joggers run past us and spit and everything would seem like it always did if someone didn't just walk by smoking a cigarette with a face mask under his chin. I tap my pocket to see if mine is still there. I've become a bit lax about wearing my mask this week as I have totally avoided close contact with others. This will change next week when I go to the bookstore to work, to say goodbye, I think. It's the end. Which I've dreaded. My time away has showed me that I had outgrown my position there and could better use my time writing and translating at home, my two real passions. I'm sad to leave a place I had spent a decade in and invested so much love in but I know it's time to move on. The question is whether the shop will continue. I hope so, for all those readers. For all those small business owners, all those community members, who don't know what will come next. I don't either, but I have some strange hope that we will come out of this much clearer. Then I realize that a lot of people would think I was crazy for saying this. But then I wonder: What would happen if we all thought like this? I then remember the original intent of the We Believe posters that the fan Paul Wong had made for Oracle Arena back in 2007. Wong, a Korean BBQ restaurant owner and longtime Warriors fan, wanted to motivate his fellow Warriors fans to in turn motivate the players. It was an idea Wong came up with to salvage the season and his marriage after he read the self-help book *The Secret*. And it did a pretty good job. We made it to the playoffs and won in the first round against the Dallas Mavericks! Which would be considered a disappointment for the Warriors now. How much times have changed. But then I look at the family setting up their picnic on the grass across from us and see how resistant we are to change forever. Perhaps things will be more subtle. If our interactions on the streets are any indication, perhaps we will be more mindful and compassionate of and toward one another. Kian has finally tired himself out from all the newness and is squirming around on my lap. I put him in the carrier. We walk out of the park, past the Japanese embassy, the Greek embassy, over the footbridge over the canal, and on to Lützowplatz. Alone with myself, I think about what I have learned and am learning and constantly reminding myself to remember. That I need to live joyfully. That I need to be mindful. That I need to have compassion. And that I need to compete for these to be real. It's a constant process that requires a lot of repetition—just like shooting a basketball with accuracy does—and

it's admittedly easy to lose sight of. I take some solace in knowing that I'm not the only one who struggles with this. The same
could be said for the current and past Warriors. Last summer,
when I interviewed Andre Iguodala about his book *The Sixth Man*
for the magazine *032c*, I asked him why Steve Kerr always talked
about joy in the media and never mentioned the other core values. Iguodala's answer was simple: joy is the easiest to forget.
Which seems insane given Western society's emphasis on happiness, but obvious if you remember that joy is a question of doing.
That you have to already act joyfully in the grind. And that you
can't pretend to believe. I walk up Maaßenstraße, past an earlier version of myself, a young man with a cigarette and beer in
his hand, and turn right on Winterfeldtstraße, then left on our
street. Kian wakes up before I unlock the door to the building—
he always does when we're home. Home. It's like he can sense
it. We walk into the courtyard where Catherine is watering the
heather and grass patch she has recently planted, I wave and walk
up the stairs. When I open the door, I hear Melanie singing in the
kitchen. She's listening to our wedding mix and my favorite Sun
Ra song is playing—"Love in Outer Space." She's trying to suppress her wide smile and from her coyness, I can tell something
is up. I ask her whether she was just preparing something for
my birthday tomorrow while we were gone. She says *no* and then
It's a secret. There's a salad on the table and the leftover omelet I
made yesterday and she needed to take a break from work anyway. We smile and kiss. You were gone for a long time, she says.
I tell her about the magnolia trees and that Kian was fascinated
by the geese. She's in a really good mood and wants to dance
with her two boys. Go wash up, she says, and then helps me to

remove Kian from the carrier to breastfeed him. Now Captain Beefheart's "I'm Glad" is playing and I sing along in a Beefheart growling crooning imitation: "When you first came around I was sad / My head hung down I felt really bad / Now I'm glad, glad about the good times that we've had." Melanie laughs. Kian and I are both excited, we want to dance too. Now hurry up, Melanie says. I go into the bathroom and turn on the tap. I wait for the water to get hot. Then I do what I always do, starting from the beginning:

Hand-washing technique with soap and water

1. Westbrook
2. Back out to Singler
3. Shot Clock at 7
4. Westbrook on the drive
5. Falling Awayyyyyy
6. Wont Go
7. Rebound taken by Iguodala
8. They do have a timeout
9. Decide not to use it
10. Curry way downtown
11. BANGGGGGGG
12. BANGGGGGGG
13. Oh what a shot from Curry

THANK YOU

As I write, the Caldor fire is raging in the Tahoe Basin, decimating forestland that's been ravaged by decades of drought and inching closer and closer to my childhood home. This is only one fire of many and there will be even more unless we address the climate crisis and learn to live more harmoniously with our surroundings, ourselves. There's a lot to be worried about and mad about and sad about but there is also much to be grateful for.

Thank you, Melanie, for being my ray of light; for bringing brightness and joy and clarity into this life that is so full of smoky obfuscation; for challenging me whenever I needed to be challenged; and for sharing your life with me. I love you very, very much. Thank you, too, for all your thoughts and suggestions regarding this never-ending manuscript, most of which I followed (and please forgive me where I didn't). We did it.

Thank you, Kian, for joining us on this journey; for bringing laughter and curiosity with you; for teaching us to slow down and immerse ourselves in the present. You're now part of the Anderson–Sehgal family and I'd like to thank all members (especially Stephanie, Duane, and Carrie; Therese, Surin, Tino, Dorothea, Nalin, and Kanya) for showing me what that word means.

And speaking of family: thank you, Will Evans, for welcoming me into the Deep Vellum clan and for taking on this unruly book that branches out like life branches out, forking and bending whenever needed. Thank you, Kirby Gann, Sara Balabanlilar, Serena Reiser, Walker Rutter-Bowman, and everyone else at Deep Vellum for cultivating this book. Thanks especially to Zac Crain for his edits, for pushing me into unfamiliar territory, and for reassuring me that I already knew the way.

Thank you, Vytautas Volbekas, for your incredible cover design and for translating the spirit of the book into a real masterpiece. I couldn't be any happier, thank you.

Thank you, CAConrad, for that life-changing conversation on the park bench. I would have never dared to write this book without your advice, thank you.

Thank you, Josh Berson, Martin Ingebrigtsen, Greg Nissan, Mathias R. Samuelsen, and Caleb Waldorf, for being the best starting five anyone could ask for, for always being willing to listen to me spin even more yarn as this thing morphed from a simple essay ("it's not really a big deal, I mean, it'll take me a month, tops") to what it is today, and for reading it so many damned times. Thank you for giving me the courage to keep going and to go even deeper.

Thank you, Aernout Mik, Alex Martinis Roe, Alicia Frankovich, Anthony Kuan, Asad Raza, Assaf Gruber, Bakri Bakhit, Blake Butler, Carson Chan, Christian Hawkey, Corina Copp, Daniel Jenatsch, Daniel Massey, Daniela Seel, Descha

Daemgen, Donna Stonecipher, Elvia Wilk, Eric Blocher, Fiona Geuß, Florian Werner, Fotini Lazaridou-Hatzigoga, Frances Kruk, Francesca Lisette, Francesca Raimondi, Frank Willens, Gideon Lewis-Kraus, Grant Kerber, Greg Kerber, Hendrik Weber, India Ennenga, Jan Kampfshoff, Jen Allen, Jennifer Nelson, Jocelyn Walker, John Holten, Jörg Albrecht, Josh Cohen, Julia Grosse, Kathrin Jira, Lotte Thiessen, Louise Höjer, Luciano Chessa, Justina Zubė, Matt Gibson, Mei Yu, Nick Horton, Nina Stark, Priscilla Posada, Rachel Valinsky, Regina de Miguel, Sam Cooney, Sam Langer, Sarah Ross, Sebastian Clark, Sjoerd Dijk, Sophia de le Fraga, Terri Young, Tevya Fetter, Thomas Pletzinger, Tina Buchen, Tzu Chien Tho, Uljana Wolf, Valentinas Klimašauskas, Virginija Januškevičiūtė, Will Alexander, Xavier Le Roy, Yashi Kunz, Zeda Samuel, and all the guys at DBC Berlin for your love and wisdom, for your insightful readings and invitations, for taking care of me when I needed taking care of, and/or for all years of getting it together in action.

Thank you, Steve Kerr, Stephen Curry, Klay Thompson, Draymond Green, Andre Iguodala, Kevin Durant, and all the Warriors, future and past, for showing me what greatness really is. I've learned a lot from your example.

Thank you to all the countless writers. A bibliography for this book seems justified but then this could only ever list all those writers who are clearly cited (and so, easily googleable) and not the myriad others whose influence can be felt despite remaining unnamed. That said, thanks to Anthony Slater, Bill Simmons, Bob Fitzgerald, Erik Malinowski, Ethan Strauss, Jim Barnett, Kelenna Azubuike, Kerith Burke, Marcus Thompson II, Monte Poole, Ros Gold-Onwude, Tim Kawakami, Zach Lowe, and all other members of the media at the *East Bay Times*, ESPN, *Mercury News*, r/warriors, *SF Gate*, *Sports Illustrated*, the *Athletic*, and the *Ringer*—without your coverage of the Golden State Warriors, this book would be full of many inaccuracies.

Speaking of which, and to switch metaphors again: this book has the occasional hole. I've done my best to mend them whenever possible, and this has sometimes required further alterations—a hem here, a patch there, another tone. All of which has been done only to protect the fabric (the people, the point, etc.) and to make it breathe, make it livable.

The first chapter, "Beginning, Again," is for Chris LaCroix; "Mindfulness" is for Sean Bonney; "Compassion" is for Dina Lammon. If you are having suicidal thoughts, thinking about hurting yourself, or are concerned that someone you know may be in danger of hurting themselves, please call the suicide prevention hotline in the country you live in. Never forget that you have the light inside. Even if you can't see it, it's there.

And remember: we can still make magic together.

Thank you for reading.

Shane Anderson is the author of three books of poetry and experimental prose and has translated three books of poetry and basketball literature. His work has appeared or will appear in *The Nation*, the *Los Angeles Review of Books*, *032c*, *Asymptote*, and elsewhere. He is the translator of Thomas Pletzinger's Spiegel Bestseller *The Great Nowitzki*, published by Norton.

Thank you all
for your support.
We do this for you,
and could not do
it without you.

DEEP
VELLUM

PARTNERS

pixel ||| texel

EMBREY FAMILY
FOUNDATION

ADDITIONAL DONORS, CONT'D

Mark Haber
Mary Cline
Maynard Thomson
Michael Reklis
Mike Soto
Mokhtar Ramadan
Nikki & Dennis Gibson
Patrick Kukucka
Patrick Kutcher
Rev. Elizabeth & Neil Moseley
Richard Meyer

Scott & Katy Nimmons
Sherry Perry
Sydneyann Binion
Stephen Harding
Stephen Williamson
Susan Carp
Susan Ernst
Theater Jones
Tim Perttula
Tony Thomson

SUBSCRIBERS

Joseph Rebella
Michael Lighty
Shelby Vincent
Margaret Terwey
Ben Fountain

AVAILABLE NOW FROM DEEP VELLUM

MICHÈLE AUDIN · *One Hundred Twenty-One Days*
translated by Christiana Hills · FRANCE

BAE SUAH · *Recitation*
translated by Deborah Smith · SOUTH KOREA

MARIO BELLATIN · *Mrs. Murakami's Garden*
translated by Heather Cleary · MEXICO

EDUARDO BERTI · *The Imagined Land*
translated by Charlotte Coombe · ARGENTINA

CARMEN BOULLOSA · *Texas: The Great Theft* · *Before* · *Heavens on Earth*
translated by Samantha Schnee · Peter Bush · Shelby Vincent · MEXICO

MAGDA CARNECI · *FEM*
translated by Sean Cotter · ROMANIA

MATHILDE CLARK · *Lone Star*
translated by Martin Aitken · DENMARK

LEILA S. CHUDORI · *Home*
translated by John H. McGlynn · INDONESIA

SARAH CLEAVE, ed. · *Banthology: Stories from Banned Nations* ·
IRAN, IRAQ, LIBYA, SOMALIA, SUDAN, SYRIA & YEMEN

ANANDA DEVI · *Eve Out of Her Ruins*
translated by Jeffrey Zuckerman · MAURITIUS

PETER DIMOCK · *Daybook from Sheep Meadow* · USA

CLAUDIA ULLOA DONOSO · *Little Bird*, translated by Lily Meyer · PERU/NORWAY

ROSS FARRAR · *Ross Sings Cheree & the Animated Dark: Poems* · USA

ALISA GANIEVA · *Bride and Groom* · *The Mountain and the Wall*
translated by Carol Apollonio · RUSSIA

ANNE GARRÉTA · *Sphinx* · *Not One Day* · *In Concrete*
translated by Emma Ramadan · FRANCE

JÓN GNARR · *The Indian* · *The Pirate* · *The Outlaw*
translated by Lytton Smith · ICELAND

GOETHE · *The Golden Goblet: Selected Poems* · *Faust, Part One*
translated by Zsuzsanna Ozsváth and Frederick Turner · GERMANY

NOEMI JAFFE · *What are the Blind Men Dreaming?*
translated by Julia Sanches & Ellen Elias-Bursac · BRAZIL

CLAUDIA SALAZAR JIMÉNEZ · *Blood of the Dawn*
translated by Elizabeth Bryer · PERU

JUNG YOUNG MOON · *Seven Samurai Swept Away in a River* · *Vaseline Buddha*
translated by Yewon Jung · SOUTH KOREA

KIM YIDEUM · *Blood Sisters*
translated by Ji yoon Lee · SOUTH KOREA

JOSEFINE KLOUGART · *Of Darkness*
translated by Martin Aitken · DENMARK

YANICK LAHENS · *Moonbath*
translated by Emily Gogolak · HAITI

FORTHCOMING FROM DEEP VELLUM

SHANE ANDERSON • *After the Oracle* • USA

MARIO BELLATIN • *Beauty Salon* • translated by David Shook • MEXICO

MIRCEA CĂRTĂRESCU · *Solenoid*
translated by Sean Cotter · ROMANIA

LOGEN CURE · *Welcome to Midland: Poems* · USA

LEYLÂ ERBIL · *A Strange Woman*
translated by Nermin Menemencioğlu · TURKEY

RADNA FABIAS • Habitus • translated by David Colmer • NETHERLANDS

SARA GOUDARZI • *The Almond in the Apricot* • USA

SONG LIN • *The Gleaner Song* • translated by Dong Li • CHINA

JUNG YOUNG MOON · *Arriving in a Thick Fog*
translated by Mah Eunji and Jeffrey Karvonen · SOUTH KOREA

FISTON MWANZA MUJILA · *The Villain's Dance,* translated by Roland Glasser
DEMOCRATIC REPUBLIC OF CONGO

JOHNATHAN NORTON • *Penny Candy* • USA

LUDMILLA PETRUSHEVSKAYA · *Kidnapped: A Crime Story,* translated by Marian
Schwartz · *The New Adventures of Helen: Magical Tales,* translated by Jane Bugaeva ·
RUSSIA

SERGIO PITOL • *The Love Parade* • translated by G. B. Henson • MEXICO

MANON STEFAN ROS · *The Blue Book of Nebo* · WALES

ETHAN RUTHERFORD · *Farthest South & Other Stories* · USA

BOB TRAMMELL · *The Origins of the Avant-Garde in Dallas & Other Stories* · USA